MW00910295

lorraine.wincor@aol.com

Dr. Lorraine Wincor
Life Coach/ Psychologist & Author
Marriage Circus 2009
Brain Matters 2015

ED 954-540-2579
(Cell

EMDR Specialist
3200 Port Royale Dr. # 1203
Ft. Lauderdale, FL 33308

Phone: (954) 772-6015
Cell: (954) 540-0977

The Marriage Circus

By Lorraine Wincor, Psy.D

INFINITY
PUBLISHING.COM

ISBN 0-7414-5383-5

Published by:

INFI(∞)ITY
PUBLISHING.COM

1094 New DeHaven Street, Suite 100
West Conshohocken, PA 19428-2713
Info@buybooksontheweb.com
www.buybooksontheweb.com
Toll-free (877) BUY BOOK
Local Phone (610) 941-9999
Fax (610) 941-9959

Printed in the United States of America

Published September 2009

Acknowledgments

First and foremost I want to thank my husband, Dr. Edward Reichbach, who has been my constant assistant and cheerleader. Without his help and patience I could not have completed this book. He hugged and encouraged me along the way during the many months it took me to write. I would also like to thank my two amazing adult children, Dr. Robert Raylove and Ms. Lyn Benjamin, who cheered me on, listened, asked questions, read scripts and offered editorial assistance. I am grateful to my granddaughter Alanna Tonelli-Raylove for designing the drawings and cover for me when she would rather have been riding horses. My neighbor Amy Blake was always there to assist me with the computer glitches, for which I am most grateful. And finally I thank the Osterville Writer's Group, who gave me input and suggestions each week with special thanks to Mr. Arthur Clarke and Dr. David Shelfin. I thank God for giving me the energy, imagination and patience to make my dream come true.

TABLE OF CONTENTS

When two people are in a committed relationship, discovering the deepest emotional desire of your partner and staying conscious of that desire, will almost guarantee a relationship without divorce. Think of that! Think of what this lifestyle will teach your children. Amen!

Romantic Stage

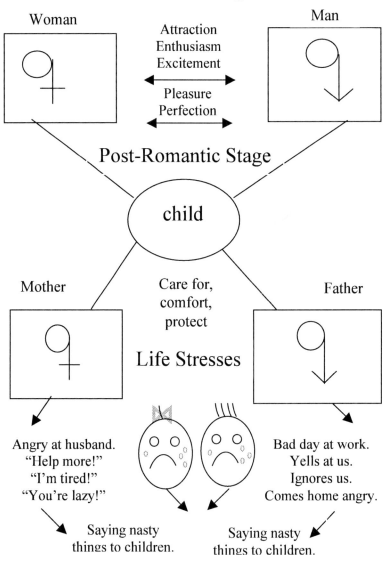

Woman

Man

Attraction
Enthusiasm
Excitement

Pleasure
Perfection

Post-Romantic Stage

child

Mother

Care for,
comfort,
protect

Father

Life Stresses

Angry at husband.
"Help more!"
"I'm tired!"
"You're lazy!"

Bad day at work.
Yells at us.
Ignores us.
Comes home angry.

Saying nasty
things to children.

Saying nasty
things to children.

"You're a slob." "You're a loser." "Only sissies cry."
"You're stupid", "lazy", "bad", "selfish".

1

CHAPTER 1

A Broken Marriage is Like a Broken Circle

(Note: The pronouns "he" and "she" are used interchangeably in this book.)

Have you ever wondered about the purpose of marriage? Why do so many people marry? What do people want? Is it societal and peer pressure? Parental pressure? Pregnancy? Loneliness? Wanting a family? Financial safety? Fear of being alone? Getting older? Wanting to change geography? Falling in love? Or, do we think it's our last chance to grow up?

What brings couples together? Is it more an unconscious need to complete ourselves by having a friend and partner? What is it we see in this person that makes us so willing and anxious to marry? What keeps us together? When love dies, is it from neglect or weariness or ignorance?

Love doesn't depend on hope – it depends on action. I propose that marital success takes effort and depends on knowledge of each other beginning with childhood. When each person gains an enriched understanding of the other and their history, new vistas of understanding open up.

Most healthy people do not want to reach the end of their lives without experiencing love. It is like breathing. We need air to breathe, and human beings need and want love in their lives. The question is, how do we get it? How do we treat love? What are the unconscious roadblocks that keep us from succeeding?

I am suggesting that we marry, without realizing it, to complete the unfinished business of childhood. By wanting to complete ourselves, we unconsciously choose as our partner a person whose traits we perceive we emotionally need and want. At an unconscious level we are attracted to someone who resembles our caretakers, for better or worse.

I do not exclude parents, who, though they do their best, cannot satisfy their child's every need. For example, a newborn infant cries and cries and cries, and no matter how hard a parent tries, she cannot always comfort him. Some parents want to be affectionate to a child but often have endless needs themselves, so despite how devoted they are, they cannot satisfy their child's needs. Many first-time parents are inexperienced and turn to the "experts" for help without using common sense.

I remember walking my firstborn all night for months after bringing him home from the hospital. No amount of comforting could quiet his distress or pain, and the doctors didn't have a clue as to what was wrong with him. This was also the era of Dr. Spock, who wrote the "bible" for new parents. The philosophy was, "if the baby is fed, clean, and burped, let him cry so you don't spoil him." So he cried and cried without receiving comfort. I would pace the floors outside the room, preventing myself from picking him up in order to follow Dr. Spock's advice. I was 18 and an inexperienced mom. What I now realize is that my baby was wounded and afraid. I often wonder how much damage was done by making these kinds of mistakes and not leading with the heart.

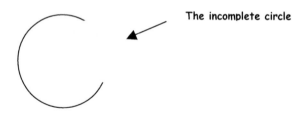

The incomplete circle

The opening in the circle represents those experiences we wanted as children: things which our caretakers, for whatever reason, were unable to provide. That missing piece hypothetically represents our unmet, unconscious emotional needs which attract us to the person(s) we marry. There is a sense that he is capable of filling us up and giving us what we so crave. We expect our spouse to take care of us. When she does not, we get angry and afraid. We unconsciously select a spouse with some of the same traits as our parents as a way to heal what has been missing since childhood. And after marrying our chosen person, we try our best to change him. We re-create our childhood script and act out with our spouse the uncomfortable scenes we experienced early in life. Here is an example:

Lori and Ted came from very different home backgrounds. Ted came from a home where his parents never complimented, encouraged, nor acknowledged that he had any talent or any abilities. He never received a hug or a kiss during his entire childhood or adolescence, that he could recall. He finally escaped by joining the army at age seventeen.

Lori came from a home where she received daily hugs and affection from her father. But her mother was an unhappy woman who always felt sorry for herself. Her mother took care of the physical needs of her youngest daughter, but was too emotionally empty herself to give more than that.

Ted married Lori and behaved as her mother had. She had wanted another loving father, and she worked and worked at trying to remake Ted into that role. He was a man who didn't know how to give, and resisted all attempts to learn. The universal humor of it is that Ted married her because she was an emotional giver, yet he played out the role of his parents.

Let's look for a moment at how these feelings might originate. The fetus, after a certain amount of time in utero, appears to be aware of sounds and to be responsive to the mother's mood and the voices around him. The baby's movements can be charted on a sonogram and his reactions interpreted. It is therefore quite possible that awareness begins before birth. The growing, unborn baby is impressionable and can respond to stimuli for months before he starts squirming in his mother's arms. By the time some infants come into the world they have already been exposed to negative impressions related to angry voices and jarring sounds.

Many children therefore come into the world with something missing in terms of feeling comfortable and satisfied. As a child grows, he has more and more experiences as he interacts with his environment – some good, and some bad. What kind of environment is the child born into? How do his senses develop?

High
vitality

Self assured

Good self
image

"You're so smart!"

"You're so pretty!"

"I love you!"

Confident, good
self-esteem.

Low vitality

Sad, depressed

Nail Biter

Anxious

Poor self image

Hyperactive

"You're so
strong,
creative,
clever."

"I never had it – why should you?"

"The boys won't like you."

"Can't do math? You're dumb."

"Why don't you ever stop growing?"

"You're too little to play
football."

What kinds of smells does he smell? Are they pleasing or upsetting? What are the sounds that he hears? Are they raucous or soothing? What kinds of sights does he see? Are they fear-producing or calming? What feelings does he feel? Is he frightened or comforted? What kinds of tastes does he experience? Are they vile or delicious? Is he born into a loving place, or a threatening and frightening place? Are the caretakers attentive or antagonistic, patient or dismissive, mentally healthy or themselves in need of care?

In this context the incomplete circle can represent the questionable positive and negative experiences in a child's early life. Every human being wants completion or closure to feel whole. For many it is a lifelong search. For some it is never achieved.

By the time we are five years old we know what our family is about. By the time we are five we know what we need and want. By the time we marry we choose the person who appears to have what we most want. Now that we have him, we think we can change our partner to give us what we crave. The unfinished circle will then be complete. However, it rarely works that way. And then there is anger and resentment.

Before the age of five children are generally outgoing, expressive and bold. However, over time, the adults around them often destroy their confidence, and the power the young ones had at birth is significantly lost. Caretakers, be they family members or others, can be detrimental to our attitudes and beliefs. This has a direct correlation on our choice of marital partner.

CHAPTER 2

Why This Therapy?

"Good relationships don't just happen: they are created"

According to my favorite form of couples therapy, called Imago, couples are attracted to their significant others because they unconsciously see in them the positive and negative traits that they experienced in their caregivers. They yearn to fulfill their own unmet emotional needs of childhood. Our unconscious purpose for getting married is to close that emotional gap in the circle and make ourselves feel whole by using our partner to give us what we missed and wanted. It is as if we are seeking to complete an unfinished puzzle by finding the missing piece.

While Freud and others after him spent years studying and writing about the effects of childhood experiences on adult emotional development, it is this therapy that recognized the effects of these experiences on the marital relationship. The importance of COUPLES sharing their childhood experiences with each other, especially when the marriage is endangered, was emphasized.

I'm a clinical psychologist, in practice for 30 years. My university training taught me to work with couples in traditional talk therapy. While I found it somewhat successful in its approach, it never seemed to reach to the heart of the problem. Something was missing, and I was unable to define it. Then, in 2000, my husband and

I decided to enroll in an Imago therapy program. Our experience created an excitement and respect for its procedures. We found a therapist to help us extend our practice sessions and this, combined with what we had already experienced, opened up for me a completely different approach to marital therapy. Since that time I have been practicing this method both personally and professionally. The respect I gained for the method made me want to share it with others.

Though in practice I added some of my own concepts, ideas and exercises, the basic approach is similar to the therapy I personally experienced years ago.

This is a learning experience that teaches us <u>how</u> to love. It supports our growth as sensitive, caring human beings. A lifetime isn't very long to learn the lesson God or the universe wants us to learn: to love ourselves and to love others. All the money, all the prestigious jobs, and all the power in the world is meaningless if love doesn't exist. If we die without having experienced love, we've missed the point of living.

One major goal of the program is to teach couples how to heal the damaged and hurt parts of themselves. Experiences with childhood caretakers often produce adult cognitive distortions, addictions and other mental aberrations. The therapy strives to repair the injuries from childhood so that people can reclaim who they were meant to be from the time of natal development. This healing allows them to experience life with more hope, enthusiasm, joy, affection and love for themselves, for their partner, and in all other relationships that have meaning in their lives.

Many of our childhood memories reside in our unconscious brain and are often lost. Unhappy memories are often denied or buried because of the pain they would arouse if remembered. Conscious and unconscious memories, nevertheless define who we are, how we behave, what we think. The good news is that we can learn from the uncovering and grow emotionally.

The theory behind the therapy I practice is that we choose our partners as a way to fill the gaps in our lives. Therapy allows us to uncover and face the unconscious parts of ourselves in a safe and supportive environment. Once the pain from our past is shared with our significant other, understood and emotionally related to, it is easier to put those memories in perspective and embrace our adult lives with compassion and love for ourselves and our partner.

This therapy does not offer a quick fix. What does work is if you do your homework in good faith: with hope, understanding, courage, trust and passion. As long as you continue the process, healing will evolve. It will work if you care about your partner and are there to help her face, not deny, old hurts. If you give up or quit, you are likely to return to the old habits of blame and defeat. When either half of a couple finds excuses not to practice the steps, they are, in essence, choosing the end of love in the relationship. Refusal to practice is the way of strangling the potential to bring love back to the marriage and of resigning responsibility for the relationship. The bottom line is that you are making a life choice: choose love instead of termination, and work the program.

If you stick with the program it will work for you, as it has for many couples who wanted their marriages to grow, mature and feel safe. It is hard work, and for some couples, too painful to achieve.

What does the word Imago mean? It originates from the Latin term for "image." There are two definitions. The first says that Imago is an insect in its final adult state: sexually mature and typically winged. The second definition is that Imago is an idealized mental image of another person or the self.

No doubt the second definition is the one intended to refer to couples therapy. However, with tongue in cheek, I can support the use of the first definition as well. It's a stretch, but try substituting "person" for "insect." Imago theory deals with sexually mature couples learning to soar in their marriages. With a little imagination, I'd like to think that both definitions apply.

Couples' therapy wants us to feel less traumatized, safer, more respected and more loving and loved. We want our partner to be for us what our parents and caretakers were not always able to be.

Waiting too long for marital counseling may be beyond redemption. The average couple waits 6 years to reach out for help, but often too much erosion has taken place. Entrenchment in ugly patterns keeps you stuck , and then it is harder to get unstuck.

The program is not a problem-solving tool. A different therapeutic environment is created. Where once there were problems in a marriage, there are now solutions.

The solutions begin when partners reveal their histories to each other and understand the impact those histories have on the way husband and wife relate to each other.

This discovery of history evolves into a conscious challenge to heal and rid oneself of all those things that depressed and terrorized us as children: the hurt, the anger, the emotional and physical abuse, the feelings of abandonment, the divorce, the absent parent, the abusive sibling, the drunken parent, the loneliness, the disappointment, the criticism, not being good enough, smart enough, pretty enough, handsome enough, tall enough, short enough, thin enough, fat enough, healthy enough. As adults some of us grew up feeling that we were missing something. Others wanted more of what they already had. Marriage, we believed, was probably the answer.

Many of us have experienced childhood fear, disappointment, wounding of the soul as children. Our caretakers, for whatever the reason, were not there to help us when we needed them. Now we have a partner. How lucky we are to have someone to hear us, understand us, comfort us, empathize with us. We no longer have to put up our walls of defense to protect us from hurt. We have a partner who is willing to listen and celebrate life with us.

The hardest years of a marriage are those following the wedding.

NEGATIVE PARENTAL MESSAGES

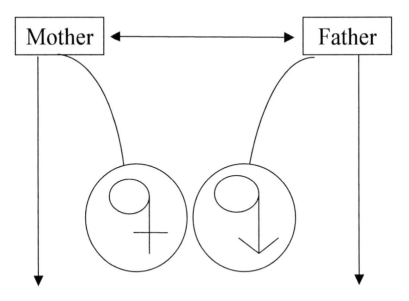

"When you're a mom, you can say nice things to your kids. Right now I'm so mad, I don't care what you think. Do what you're told – **NOW**!"

"Don't do what I do, do what I say!" "I hope your kids are as rotten, bad, sloppy and fresh as you are."

These messages are examples of psychological insults. They often damage children's self-esteem, especially because the messages are delivered by the adults who raised them.

CHAPTER 3

Is Romantic Love the Answer?

Before we learn how the challenging task of completion is achieved, let's review. The open space in the circle needs to be closed, and we meet this challenge by choosing our marriage partner. Why him? Why her? The answer is often, "I'm not sure. There was just something..." The opening represents the pluses and minuses of the behavior of the people who raised us. We see something in our marital choice that unconsciously suggests this is the one who can make us happy: someone who will bring us satisfaction and contentment. We often want our partners to be our personal coach and trainer.

Many people keep repeating the process from one relationship to the next – always searching for the pot of gold, only to find it empty. "What happened to the woman I married, the man I married?" is the cry often heard. People don't get married to take care of their partner's needs: they marry to further their own psychological and emotional growth. The negative traits come to the fore following the romantic stage, when it sometimes feels like your partner is hurting you the same way you were hurt as a child. As romantic love begins to disappear our partners stop making us feel better; instead we start to emotionally re-injure each other. That is followed by projecting our negative traits onto each other and starting to blame each other for the negative traits within ourselves. This is one way we defend ourselves. (More about this later.)

Falling IN love is fun. Being in love is easy. It emits more energy and is more romantic than working through the problems of a marriage.

And what about the role of chemicals during the initial attraction of the Romantic Stage? Brain Chemicals can't be ignored. At the first meeting and early thereafter during this stage, couples focus only on each other's qualities. Negative qualities aren't even noticed! It's called lust. The bottom line is chemicals operating in the brain placed there, no doubt, by the universe or God or whatever you choose to call something much bigger than yourself. They are there for a purpose, and that purpose is reproduction. Chemicals have every-thing to do with what is felt in the beginning of a "hot" relationship.

Dopamine makes you feel good. Phenylecthylamine raises your excitement. Seratonin makes you feel stable. Norepinephrine makes you think you can achieve anything you want. Remember, a man's brain is controlled by his testosterone level at this stage.

The Romantic Stage lasts for about a year , perhaps a little longer. As the dynamics of the stage wanes, the testosterone level begins to slow, and the married couple often then begins to think that having a child will accelerate the excitement again.

Many of us think that by starting afresh with a new partner that we will do things differently this time. After all, our new partner is different: we made certain of that. Yet in some unfathomable way he may not help us to close that gap in the circle. What isn't understood is that each partner is struggling to close his own gap.

Once we are married we exhaust ourselves trying to change our partner so that she will meet our needs and complete us, while at the same time our partner is exhausting himself in the same unsuccessful way. The outcome is frustration, anger, rejection, and disappointment. One woman I worked with succeeded in changing her husband and then complained, "What happened to the man I married?"

Romantic love and the struggle that follows have one thing in common: neither will make each partner complete. Neither will fill in the missing piece. Before that can happen we have to become aware of what our unconscious holds, and share it with our spouse.

Before marriage we were blind to our lover's faults and saw only the positives. We appeared to love through blinders. In those times, when something negative emerged during this romantic period we tended to overlook or minimize our feelings. We thought it would change after the wedding. When we remarry the new partner may look differently, act differently, and be educated differently, yet something about each is similar. That is what attracted us.

I know, because it happened to me in my second marriage.

The wedding plans were in place, the invitations were sent, and the deposit on the venue was made. Then, for the first time since we'd met, my fiancé exploded with an anger so intense that he threatened to cancel the wedding. It scared me, and I panicked. Quickly placating him (after all I AM a psychologist) I apologized for something I had said which was the alleged trigger. At that moment he was unapproachable. I was surprised and puzzled. What I didn't understand at that time was that the source of his outrage was hurt. Without knowing it, I had triggered a childhood injury. Whatever that injury was, it was part of the gap in his circle. I learned at the workshop where that hurt originated.

Another example can be seen in a young couple who came to see me about their marriage of six years. She was extraordinarily sensitive about being left alone. In taking her history I learned that her biological father had committed suicide when she was three years old. Her mother remarried shortly after and spent most of her time with her new husband, leaving her daughter with babysitters. The stepfather, she said, was dismissive and loud. The patient felt frightened and abandoned.

My patient married a sweet, caring, intelligent young man who loved her. However his job required him to work long, late hours. His mother was ill, and he visited her after work two or three nights a week, leaving his wife alone. She complained about his visits to see his mother and was sure he loved his job and his mother more than he loved her. Once he understood what her abandonment issues were they were able to be more trusting and sensitive toward each other; to communicate their plans and agree to schedules. The husband had no concept of how hurt she was from her childhood deprivations. Until he understood the connection between her childhood abandonment, his late working hours and his visits several times a week to see his mother, he was unable to empathize with her.

Many of us get mixed messages as children. Things we hold onto as we age affect the way we think about ourselves. Ideas buried in our unconscious often reflect our choices of marriage partners.

Some children think they are "bad" or "ugly" or "stupid" or "unloved" as a result of things they've been told or the way they have been treated by caretakers, teachers, siblings or playmates. These negative messages lead to false beliefs about ourselves which can cause symptoms that damage our minds and bodies. Anchoring negative childhood messages in our brain can become our mantra and lifetime habit. We unconsciously anchor, and it infects our relationships and keeps us depressed. It's as if a virus has been planted in your brain computer which keeps spreading and spreading until a breakdown of mind, body and spirit occurs. The good news is that brain surgery isn't necessary. Instead, an alternative way of programming your thinking can change your life.

A true example of negative childhood messages came from one of my patients in describing her childhood experience.

Carla was the youngest child of three female siblings. Her parents told her they had wanted a son, and seven years after the second sister was born they tried for another child. Carla was born.

Her parents were disappointed about having another girl. As Carla grew up, her father worked long hours as a civil servant on the police force, and she was left alone with her non-working mother. Her mother cooked a lot and never involved Carla in the process.

Mama talked incessantly on the telephone to her girlfriends, completely ignoring Carla for hours at a time. Carla, before school age, would ask for her mother's attention only to be told, "Go bang your head against the wall." She heard this many times in her early childhood. This made her angry and resentful, yet to be accepted she became the "good" child. Watching her older sister act out and get threatened with the strap was another motivation to be good.

Carla became a shy, nail-biting, overweight child who tried and tried and tried to be as good as she could be. But nothing she did seemed to gain approval or affection from her mother. She internalized her depression and anger to protect herself. She wouldn't dare express it openly. Once, in second grade, she stole some jewelry from under a classmate's desk. Through a process of elimination she was caught, humiliated in front of the class, and punished. Unconsciously she hoped her mother would feel embarrassment at having a thief for a daughter and give her some attention. It wasn't until she was a teenager that Carla began to have a few friends: she was used to functioning as a loner.

Carla's childhood wounds originated because she had an unhappy mother who was not able to love or show her affection. Carla's grandmother died at thirty-five leaving her daughter, a teenager, in charge of an angry drunken father who never had a nice word for his daughter. At nineteen Carla married a man her parents disapproved of, had a baby eleven months later, and expected her husband, a needy man himself, to meet her enormous emotional needs.

You may be saying to yourself "Who goes around dwelling on this stuff after all these years? Get over it! Childhood was a long time ago. Don't dwell on negatives. Be joyful and count your blessings." But that is like telling a poor man to pull himself up by his bootstraps when he has no boots. We don't automatically "get over it" when we don't understand how and why it all began. Many of these memories are unconscious. Nothing changes until there is awareness and it is brought to the surface. Change must be preceded by awareness, and therapy teaches couples to become aware and reinterpret their life experiences.

Awareness of our condition may not exist in the forefront of our conscious mind, yet the feelings related to those early experiences remain in our unconscious and are re-experienced in our behaviors as adults. Whether or not we are conscious of our history, our needs, and why we are uncomfortable, we never stop yearning for completion. I am talking about the unconscious mind – the mind that holds the secrets of our past, the mind that harbors memories of which we are not aware during our day-to-day lives. Sometimes when we are hypnotized, engaged in deep relaxation, practicing imagery or dreaming, the memories are released. Most of the time, however, the memories are repressed and denied because they are too painful to look at.

Below is an actual experience of how a thirty-five year old patient released a repressed memory from age five, while participating in a group session at my office with seven other women.

Tina was a pretty woman, single and very overweight. This was our first meeting, and she told me she had never been hypnotized before. She was highly motivated to see if she could be. The process took about forty minutes. At its completion, each person was asked to share her experience.

The first words from Tina were, "Oh my God-now I understand." She held the group's attention as she related the following.

"All of my life, I have been fat. I have tried every diet for years and years, only to experience failure. This is what I saw under hypnosis."

"I was sitting in my little chair. I was four or five years old. My parents were fighting in the next room: screaming and yelling at each other. I was scared, and I rocked back and forth faster and faster. I covered my ears, but it wouldn't stop. I saw myself drag the chair over to the cupboard, stand on it, open the cupboard door and take down the jar of cookies. I sat down again and started to stuff my mouth with cookies. My father and mother were still screaming. I finished lots and lots of cookies. Then my mother came in, and when she saw what I had done, she slapped me hard across my face, and I cried. Then everything seemed dark."

There was a surprised look on Tina's face. "Now I can understand why I'm so fat and why diets don't work for me. The cookies were a substitute for the love I wanted just as food is now."

Consciously or not, human beings never stop wanting what we think and feel we need. This striving is part of being human and productive. It is the way we approach that striving that sometimes undermines us after we marry. We may want to be "fixed," but the bottom line is that each of us has to do our own work.

The best of marriages needs continuing thought and nurturing.

CHAPTER 4

Choosing Partners

For one human being to love another: that is the most difficult of all out tasks; the work for which all other work is but preparation: Ranier Maria Relke

Though we may joke about opposites attracting, few of us are aware that we unconsciously choose partners who either positively or negatively imitate our childhood caretakers. Until we understand this process we are destined to search for someone to fulfill our unmet needs, only to be disappointed again.

What's under the confident exterior? Is it abandonment issues because our parents divorced? Did they both work, and we were latchkey kids? Were parents depressed and angry? Something else? So-we cover it up and our partner never really knows why we act the way we do sometimes or what we need from her, because we haven't shared that information about ourselves. Is it shame based? Anger based? Why haven't we talked about it?

One intelligent and educated woman I treated had been married twice. She chose men she felt were different from each other. Husband #1 was brilliant at making decisions, had a photographic memory and was successful in business. After they were married she discovered he was also secretive and manipulative. He made all her decisions and rarely asked for an opinion. He kept my patient on edge much of the time.

She learned that his mother, a nurse, was a horrendous critic and gave him no affection. He sought an admiring, loving, attentive woman. Husband #2 was a retired professor who had traveled the world. He was bright, social, physically healthy and a good listener – certainly different from the first. However, like her first husband, he had great difficulty showing warmth. His childhood was filled with parental arguing, criticism and physical abuse. He unconsciously sought a caring, attentive partner who initially showered him with affection.

Why did this woman make those choices? It is obvious that her choices were grounded in emotionally needy men who themselves had not been nurtured as children. Unconsciously she wanted to fix them. Her father was a loving, affectionate man married to a depressed, critical woman. My patient was 65 before she understood that she was attracted to emotionally needy men like her father. She was unconsciously giving her deceased father, whom she loved, the caring and attention he deserved by showering feelings on her two husbands. In doing so she deprived herself of her own needs. Her first husband was a substitute for her critical and depressed mother.

Her big "aha" moment came to her consciousness while she was doing yoga exercises. It was then that she decided to do something about it and called for an appointment. The therapy changed her and her husband's lives. But it took time. It was not a quick fix. It taught them about unmet childhood needs and a more effective and loving way to communicate with each other. They began to appreciate the gift they had been given in helping each other to heal. They left behind criticism, hostility and paranoia. It was never perfect. The anger each felt still arose to the surface on occasion, yet they had learned what they had to do to keep it from erupting as it once had. They are friends and companions now, instead of adversaries.

The more intense the feelings and reactions in choosing your partners, the more likely you are responding to what you wanted from your own parents.

CHAPTER 5

Why Do Opposites Attract?

The cliché referring to opposites attracting is often true.

Unconsciously selecting your opposite is a way to close that open space in the circle: the space that represents those unmet needs of childhood.

Let's look at a few examples of how this process works. These are real people whose names have been changed, and their histories are true.

Try to guess what kind of partner, someone in the examples below, might choose. Put yourself in their shoes, and decide if you agree with their choices.

Situation #1: The Lonely Child

This child isn't noticed much within her family. She comes from a large family of six brothers and two sisters. She is somewhere in the middle. Her parents are always working or on call. They are either at their successful store or travelling for business reasons. When they are home, they have hobbies in which they engage for social and business purposes.

Our subject's name is Joy. She was often teased by her brothers. Joy felt little affection coming from her siblings. She reports feeling lost, unloved and unimportant. As Joy reached adolescence, she felt inadequate in spite of her good grades in school. She overate and was then teased for being "fat".

In her attempts to become noticed and accepted, she became a "helper", always putting other peoples' needs before her own. Joy displays behavior that is sometimes referred to as, "monkey mind", constantly moving here and there, rarely relaxing and always thinking about what she needs to do next. When people ask her for help, she never says, "no" for fear of once again being ignored or rejected. As an adult she is exhausted, always trying to please others.

What might her first choice of a marriage partner be?

a. _____A quiet man, with few friends, who always wants to be taken care of

b. _____An affectionate man who shares his ideas and listens to her point of view

c. _____A man who loves to stay home, read and watch t.v.

d. _____All of the above

Situation #2 The Disrespected Child

In this family, parents are present but don't spend time listening to John's requests or giving him feedback when he talks to them. There is minimal conversation directed to or about him. When he asks for something, partly to get their attention, he is told, "I don't have time for that just now", "You don't need it", "Find something else to do", "We'll think about it".

Parents of this ilk don't regard this child as a contributing part of the family conversation. John sometimes wonders if he really belongs to this family. He remembers asking, "Was I adopted?"

When John grows up and falls in love, what type of personality do you think he finds attractive?

a. _____Someone who is successful, independent and has strong opinions
b. _____Someone who holds a good job and is rarely home
c. _____A quiet person who is a good listener and shares some of his interests
d. _____All of the above

Situation #3 The Criticized Child

He is the oldest son. Tim has a younger sister and brother. His mother is the housekeeper, while the father works installing glass in an auto shop. Money is tight and budgets are lean. Tim is often expected to help care for his siblings and to assist his mother with errands and cleaning the apartment. He is often criticized for not being perfect, and although he is bright in school, he is rarely acknowledged or complimented for his good grades.

In relating his history, Tim mentions that he has never seen or heard his parents express affection for each other.

As an adult, what kind of woman would you guess he chooses for a partner?
a. _____A partner who engages in conversation with him about his work and who shares responsibility in day to day living arrangements
b. _____An attractive woman who is intelligent, has a good job and holds strong opinions about people, places and things.

c. _____A person who has many friends and keeps him busy with social engagements and chores
d. _____None of the above

Situation #4 The Rejected Child
Marlene was beautiful! She was tall, blond, blue-eyed with much positive energy. She was rarely without a date in her teens and twenties, yet did not marry until age 30. As a middle child, with an above average I.Q., she was in direct competition with her equally attractive older sister. In their teens her sister wanted to become a doctor. Marlene quit high school in the tenth grade.

Marlene's parents always asked, "Why can't you be like your older sister?" In response, Marlene broke all of the family rules. At age 18 she ran away from home and joined a religious group she knew her family would object to.

A few years went by without any family contact. Then her younger sister found out where Marlene lived and asked her to come home. When Marlene said she would, the younger sister mediated and convinced the parents that their middle daughter really wanted to return to the family home. By then the older sister was married and out of the house.

Shortly after returning home, Marlene was introduced to a divorced man. He was a successful, small businessman, owned his own home, came from an educated family with a mother who was a repressed, rigid and critical widow. When Joe asked Marlene to marry him, her family rejoiced.

What do you think were her unconscious reasons for accepting?
a. _____He was baldheaded and attentive
b. _____He was approving and anxious to marry her
c. _____She was almost thirty
d. _____As a divorced man, he was experienced

Situation #5 The Unloved Child
Raynie was emotionally ignored by her mother for most of her childhood. She craved attention and grew up feeling lonely. She wanted hugs and kisses from her mother, and these were never given.

Raynie married Jimmie. He was educated, sociable, loved to travel and was responsive to her affections. As a child Jimmy was physically and emotionally abused. He grew up angry. At an unconscious level Raynie wanted a friend and constant companion. The unconscious message was, "Show me affection"; "pay attention to me". Jimmy never wanted to be criticized again.

After they married, he heard her neediness as criticism, and his anger erupted openly, sometimes with a harsh voice and at other times by withdrawing from her for hours. He felt safer with strangers who made no emotional demands.

How do you think they resolved this situation?
a. _____Raynie learned to monitor her language and requests in a softer voice
b. _____Jimmy remembered to give her at least one hug a day

c. _____They shared each other's histories to better understand each other
d. _____All of the above

Do you think these choices we make in choosing our partners are conscious and planned? Probably not!
Once each partner understand his spouse' history and realizes what unmet needs lie in that unfinished circle, the marriage has a far better chance of improving.

How many of us have said to our best friend, "My spouse is so different from me. Why can't he be like me or my best friend? Why does he have to be so stubborn, so angry, so impatient, so disinterested, such a poor listener, so unavailable?"

And as illogical as it may sound, that is exactly why we were attracted to him, unconsciously of course- to fill in the needs gap. We chose that partner because she is like one of our caretakers: the person you loved and hated or loved and resented at the same time. You chose her to work through the trauma and disappointments of childhood. We go wrong by trying to force that person to change and give us what we so badly crave, because the forcing produces exactly what we don't want: criticism, avoidance and hostility.

Remember that these are not always conscious choices. The woman with the soft, gentle side is a comforting choice. The likelihood, however, is that when the romantic phase of the relationship is over the partner will begin to see some unattractive qualities that remind him of the childhood home. That is where this therapy does its work. It teaches us how to relate the past with what is undermining the marriage now.

I recently worked with a couple in their thirties, both of whom carried with them extremely difficult childhood histories. The wife was kind, considerate, caring and attractive. The husband was critical, negative, uncooperative and angry. Nothing the wife could do would make him budge. When she reached out to him, he rejected her. When she spoke quietly to him and requested something that was reasonable, he exploded.

The one emotional asset he had was his love for his two young children, ages three and five. After several months in therapy, without making any progress, he was finally reached when he was told how his behavior was damaging his children's future happiness. This patient was taking out all of his childhood hostility on his wife. He was seeing her as his hostile, loveless, aggressive mother. All of his energy was directed at converting her into his mother's role. That was what he was used to. That is what his experience taught him: that he wasn't worth loving. He didn't deserve to be loved. He had learned to function that way. Finally, he was able to understand how he was undermining any hope of receiving love and affection from his wife. Finally he saw quite clearly how he was ruining his children's chances for a future that included healthy marriages. Finally, he committed himself to work the program at least four times a week, to do the exercises and to ask his wife for easy gifts like two hugs a day. Now there was hope.

1. B   3. A   5. D
2. C   4. B

CHAPTER 6

Marriage Lessons

Defining Spirituality. Spirituality is a gift given us at conception. It represents the miracle of our existence. Spirituality incorporates the idea that we: you and I are a small part of a larger whole.

You've heard it said that if a bad experience didn't teach you a lesson you are supposed to learn, the universe will repeat the lesson. Reincarnation theory teaches something similar: learn the lesson you need to learn in this lifetime, or you will return again and again until the lesson is learned.

Whether you are a religious person, an agnostic, or a spiritual believer, please mull this over and consider the concept. In the context we are talking about, it is important to learn the lesson, or you will repeat the mistakes of the past over and over. Unless, of course, you are a person who believes only in chance.

This is what happens with couples. They marry and often do not get their childhood needs fulfilled. When those needs are not met, 50% of them divorce, usually in the first seven years. They are then attracted to another person who often disappoints them. The new partner may look different, have a different personality, a different education and a better job, but he may have an energy level and character that doesn't meet his spouse's needs. Again there is disappointment and frustration. Again criticism and anger are expressed.

Of the 50% of married couples who stay together, they often do so for some of the same reasons they married in the first place: societal pressures, children, financial convenience, peer pressures, fear of loneliness, getting older, family pressures, fear of abuse, health issues, and convenience. But where is the love?

People want safety and passion in their lives. You can't have one without the other. Yet when people feel safe <u>and</u> comfortable they nurture their mates. It's like throwing a stone in a pond and watching the ripples spread further and further into an extended circle. That is what happens to marriages when people are conscious, caring, courteous, expressive, complimentary, and communicative. It creates a ripple effect for the good.

If you are asking yourself, "what is the point of getting married?" the answer is to learn the lesson you need to learn about yourself for the purpose of growing up and feeling happier. It is my belief that the unconscious mind is very powerful. The universe wants us to learn that lesson and heal ourselves. But sometimes we've got to give it a little help.

Couples therapy takes us down a different path, and it is the consistency of the practice that heals us and the relationship. Criticism is never constructive when it is delivered in a hostile, blaming, attacking fashion.

Sometimes it is delivered as if it is meant to be helpful. However, it is not heard that way! Instead there is a way of getting your message across in a manner that expresses caring and is not demeaning. Criticism and fault-finding have no place in a healthy marriage. There is no such thing as helpful criticism. Love doesn't degrade. Love builds self-worth. The healing is accomplished without criticism and without insults.

The way we speak to each other changes the interaction between two needy people. Until we learn to listen and come from a place of understanding and empathy, the relationship will not change for the better. The old brain chooses our partner, but the new brain urges us to work on improving the incomplete parts of ourselves. It is astonishing to hear how many men and women describe the traits of their parents and spouses in similar terms, and those descriptions are generally negative. We try so hard to finish our unfinished work, but until we had the tools we didn't know how.

We are learning to grow up and recognize that each person has individual responsibility in the relationship and that it is necessary to affirm our significant other's point of view and feelings. The program recognizes that we are not mind readers: we need to let our partner know what we need and want. Affirming that your partner needs to feel safe and protected is a gift you give him, and you will receive loving rewards and affection in return.

Religion teaches us that it is better to give than to receive. By giving to your partner you <u>do</u> receive. You cease setting yourself up for the failure that results from blaming and criticizing. Loving relationships are not a matter of "if you do this, I'll do that." Relationships are rarely 50-50. Sometimes she gives more, but sometimes she needs more. Finding the right partner is not the key. It is <u>being</u> the right partner that pays off.

Religion, metaphysics and spirituality teach us that the universe expects us to grow and mature over time. These teach us to shed our disappointments and pain and to reach our highest levels. It is written throughout the scriptures of every religion that God and the universe wants us to achieve our greatest potential. We choose our partners to meet that challenge, although we may not be consciously aware of it. From my perspective the therapy suggests the universe has given us our partners as a gift to learn what we need to learn in order to mature and be fulfilled.

When I married Mr. Right, I didn't know his first name was always.

CHAPTER 7

Our Old and New Brain

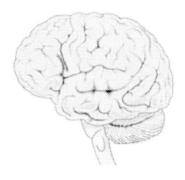

Let's look at a simplified drawing of the human brain. To better understand how the brain influences our behavior and where some of our behaviors originate, I am introducing two parts of the brain: one from the primitive or "old brain," and one from the cerebral cortex or "new brain." Through this you will understand why not everyone entering therapy is necessarily a promising candidate. Success is never guaranteed. There are factors outside of the control of good marital therapy that impede success. One of these factors involves the physical brain.

The brain has two cerebral hemispheres: one on the right and one on the left. Within one hemisphere is the primitive or "old" brain, of which the limbic system is part. The limbic system evolved early in human history and is thought to be the seat of the unconscious, instinctive behavior which is comparable to animal response. It is there to alert us to danger. The healthy limbic system plays an important role in instincts and memory, thus it holds in its unconscious the negative memories of childhood. Damage to it can increase adult negative thinking and negative perceptions of both past and current events. A person who is always pessimistic and who is flooded with negative emotions may have a faulty limbic system. When this part of the brain is overworked, emotions usually appear negative. But regardless of whether it is healthy or injured, the limbic system influences a marriage that is in trouble.

It must be apparent that someone with a faulty limbic system would not make a promising therapy candidate. Inflexible thinking and an "I don't care" attitude do not enhance good communication. Furthermore, this type of patient is uncooperative, argues for the sake of arguing and will not let go of past hurts. By virtue of being part of the primitive brain and its functioning, even a "normal" limbic system makes it difficult to work with clients who want to run away when they sense danger, or are easily hurt and frustrated. This is a recapitulation of the childhood disappointments and hurt which are buried in the unconscious old brain.

Innate primitive behaviors are modified by the new brain, or cerebral cortex. Planning for the future, and feeling hope, joy, and remorse are influenced by this part of the brain. Someone with a healthy frontal lobe has the ability to see options from which to choose or, said another way, is able to adapt to new situations. That person has the ability to learn a new way of doing things and can shift attention when it is necessary. This person would likely be a good candidate for therapy.

Problems with the frontal lobe include holding onto hurts of the past, arguing without letting go, being uncooperative and having cognitive inflexibility. This could prevent therapeutic concepts from being accepted.

Here is an example of how the old and new brain works in an adverse situation.

John is outside mowing the lawn when the rain starts. His wife Carol has just mopped the kitchen floor. John runs into the kitchen to escape the downpour. Carol impulsively screams at him that he is dragging in mud on his shoes. John feels that he is the culprit who is being verbally attacked. His old brain controls his response to his wife: "You saw the rain. Why'd you pick that time to mop? Use your brain next time and don't be so stupid." Now they are off and running, screaming at each other.

However, when the new brain is operating, the scenario would look something like this:

John is outside in the garden mowing the lawn when the sky opens up and there is a sudden downpour of rain. He runs into the kitchen to get out of the rain. His wife is just finishing up mopping the floor. She says, "Oh, don't slip. I just mopped the floor. Let me put a cotton rug down so you can take your shoes off and not slip or muddy up the floor." John responds, "Thanks honey, I should have taken my shoes off before I came in. I wasn't thinking."

Instead of defending themselves by blaming, they drop their defenses and remain friends. And the messages are exchanged in a non-threatening, friendly manner coming from the new brain and not the primitive brain.

The lesson here is that we should exchange something old and outmoded for something new that works better. Open another door. We may be programmed by our past, yet we have dreams for our future. Imagine a future with your spouse based on positive energy – energy that doesn't feel lost in the same old mistakes of the past. Couples therapy gives you a vision for the future, a way of fulfilling your partnership dreams. Your mission is clear, and that is why you are reading this book. It requires dedication, practice and a commitment to succeed.

Achieving emotional attachment to your partner will require dedication and lots of practice. Leave procrastination and blame aside and move into action. Practice, practice, practice is essential. Deepen your intimacy and rebirth yourself. You are a whole person. No one has to fix you. Be ready to face your past demons and let them go. Start using strategies that will take you where you want to go and give you what you say you want. Wishing won't make it so, and wants require action. Climb outside the box you have been restricted to for so long, and begin your new journey.

CHAPTER 8

Four Concepts Necessary to Master

Before I explain specific therapeutic methods, there are four concepts it is essential we understand about ourselves. If the process is going to succeed, it is necessary to know something about Defense Mechanisms, Cognitive Distortions, Points of View and Exits. I will briefly describe them below, then go into greater detail later in this chapter.

Defense Mechanisms

The first concept is Defense Mechanisms. From early childhood, we use defense mechanisms to protect ourselves. As children we are vulnerable and generally unable to protect ourselves, especially if we are physically, emotionally or spiritually insulted. If we are yelled at, misunderstood, ignored, berated, criticized, abandoned, or left alone, we use our defense mechanisms to help us survive. In order to remain safe and protect ourselves from vulnerability, we remain guarded and refuse to take any chances. As we grow up we continue to use our defenses – both the ones we used as children and additional ones we learn along the way that are perhaps more sophisticated. However, when we use them against our partner we further corrode and undermine the relationship. Our guardedness leads us to choose loneliness.

Point of View

The second therapeutic concept is Point of View. By gaining a point of view, couples can disagree without having to lose face and prove that one is right and one is wrong. What's the good of winning an argument if, in the end, we've made our point and lost the love? Was the ego gratification that important? Is the loneliness that enriching? What's the satisfaction worth to you? There is no perfect marriage partner. Even good marriages require not being always right. Sometimes partners in good marriages defend opposite positions and then blame the spouse. After all we began the relationship with different caretakers, different models and different histories. There are always some annoyances in the way couples relate. However, I am talking about learning to be non-critical. The process is love-fulfilling. It means letting go of anger and fear while moving closer to love. When we solve problems together we change ourselves.

Cognitive Distortions

The third concept refers to Cognitive Distortions, or the way we sometimes incorrectly think and interpret our experiences. An example of this is black-and-white thinking. When you shrank your blouse after putting it in hot water did you berate yourself and call yourself stupid? Or did you forgive yourself and move on?

Exits

The fourth concept is Exits, or escape routes. There is a difference between escaping from each other by intentionally avoiding each other, versus having separate interests. One older couple I know has the latter. He spends three or four hours a day on the computer checking stocks. She spends about the same time writing stories on her computer. On some days they share what they've created. Two people don't have to merge entirely because they are married.

Common Defense Mechanisms

By looking in more detail at some of the common defense mechanisms we can see how effective they are for the individual who uses them, and how frustrating they can be to the partner. When both spouses become aware of how and when their own defense mechanisms are used, they improve their ability to honestly communicate with each other.

Below are some defense mechanisms with examples of how they might be used. Try to identify the ones you most often use, especially when you feel cornered. Remember that defense mechanisms are used out of frustration and anxiety. We try to protect ourselves at a very early age by unconsciously employing them. While defense mechanisms don't eliminate stress, they temporarily help us to tolerate the stress and save face. All of us use defense mechanisms from time to time. They only become "bad" when we use them too often. The mechanism can become habitual and part of our personality script. Most of us aren't aware that this is happening. The problem with using defense mechanisms is that it cuts off problem-solving and communication because no one is listening. They are too busy making excuses and running away.

In service to our own growth let's look at this common list and identify which ones you call into action when you feel threatened. Once you are aware of those you own and realize how they work or don't work, you can choose to drop them from your repertoire. First however, you have to become aware of how you operate before there is change. Without awareness first, change doesn't happen. Use of a defense mechanism is habitual only because we have been using them since childhood. Become aware of when and how often you use your defenses and then you can begin to catch yourself using them. It then becomes a matter of choice as to whether you want to drop them or continue to cut off healthy communication. Let's look now at defenses we have used, some from early childhood, to protect ourselves:

Displacement: Tom's boss yells at him. He goes home and yells at his wife.

Scapegoating: You are angry at your life. Your marriage isn't working. Your bills aren't being paid. You don't like your job. So you blame a group of people who have nothing to do with your situation and who can't defend themselves (welfare recipients, blacks, Muslims, Jews, foreigners).

Identification: You come from an abused home and you are angry. You identify with a person or group you think can protect you. One example is that you join a street gang. Now you feel powerful and protected by becoming one of them. Another example would be that you have no friends so you join one of the armed forces to be part of a unified team.

Fantasy: You daydream a lot to get your secret wishes fulfilled. As a child without friends, you identify with a Hollywood star or a singer.

Denial: "Not me! I never said that, did that, saw that." This one begins at a very early age. Remember the two-year-old who looks you straight in the eye and says "me not do it!" As an adult it goes, "I NEVER promised to do that. You're lying."

Avoidance: This is related to exits. You avoid communication by engaging in an isolated activity like T.V., internet games, reading or shopping. It's an escape route.

Projection: You blame someone who has nothing to do with the situation. "If it weren't for your mother..." You hide your own anger at your wife by blaming your mother-in-law.

Regression: You revert to childhood behavior as a way to escape responsibility. "I can't, I have a stomach-ache," or "I have a headache."

Rationalization: "I work late every night, and after work I drink, because I am unhappy in the marriage." Or "if you were a better husband I wouldn't drink."

Overcompensation: A wife covers up her hostility by being the "good" wife. As a child she was nagged and nagged about picking up her toys and putting them away. Now as an adult she is a fanatic about organization at home. She wears herself out and is jealous that her husband is so relaxed, and she is always tired. "Why don't you help me more with the house? Why do I have to do everything?"

Intellectualization: You defend your position based on what you heard on T.V., saw on the internet, read in a book or heard in a lecture. What you heard, saw or read is right, and she is wrong. You are supporting your position with the "experts".

There you have it. Do you recognize yourself? Get busy and make a list with an example of your defense mechanisms and how you use them to your own advantage but to the disadvantage of your spouse and good communication.

Cognitive Distortions

Cognitive beliefs can distort a marital relationship. If Mary tells Jon over breakfast that she has a pain in her big toe, Jon may remain silent and keep eating. Mary, as a child, was ignored at home. In her house children should be seen and not heard. She responds to Jon with hurt feelings. He can't understand why. "After all, what did I say?" he asks. Mary is exaggerating and negatively interpreting Jon's disinterest in her toe because of her childhood experience. This is a form of cognitive distortion.

Below is a list of other cognitive distortions. These are related to how we think about situations based on feelings, decisions we make, opinions we have, behaviors we engage in, and choices we make. The majority of cognitive distortions began in childhood. They are not true.

Select the ones with which you can identify. Think about how you have distorted situations in your life based on your false beliefs. Think about how those beliefs have deprived you of positive outcomes.

Remember not to use the defense mechanism of denial as you look at yourself.

Write down a couple of examples from your life. This can be scary stuff when you realize how easily false beliefs can influence our behavior and our lives.

1. **"Should" thinking**: This occurs when you consistently tell yourself, "I should" in order to motivate yourself to do something (if you don't, you think you will be punished). The results are feelings of guilt. When you tell others "they should" it comes from anger and resentment.

2. **Catastrophizing**: You exaggerate the importance of things or you minimize them until they feel unimportant. For example "it was awful," or "I thought I would die," or "it was nothing," or "it was no big deal."

3. **Emotional Reasoning**: I feel it therefore it must be true. You are allowing your feelings to direct your life. <u>You</u> are in charge of your feelings. First you think it; then you feel it. Change your thinking and the feelings will follow.

4. **Jumping To Faulty Conclusions**: Though there is no real proof, you still choose to interpret a situation negatively. There are no real facts to support your conclusions. For example, you conclude that "he doesn't like me", because he didn't call. You didn't check as to why he didn't call. You are not a mind reader, and faulty conclusions can cause unnecessary emotional pain.

5. **Mentally Filtering**: This is when you color everything black because of a single negative incident, then dwelling on it, so that the reality is dark all of the time. "I lost my job, and I'm never going to find another one!"

6. **Overgeneralization**: You see one negative event as an indication of an ongoing pattern of defeat. "My husband is angry, and he left the house. I am sure he is going to divorce me."

7. **All-or-Nothing Thinking**: You see everything in shades of only black or white. For example, if you are unable to accomplish one task, you see yourself as a complete failure. "If I don't get straight A's in my major, I will never be successful in my chosen field."

8. **Disqualifying the Positive**: When something positive happens you say it doesn't count. By doing this you are able to maintain a negative belief about yourself. You get a promotion, and you say to yourself, "I'm not really qualified. I didn't deserve it."

9. **Personalization**: You see yourself as the cause of a negative event, when in fact you were not responsible for its occurrence. "If I were a better mother, my son wouldn't be using pot."

10. **Labeling**: You describe all occurrences with emotional and inappropriate language such as "I'm just a failure" or "he's a moron."

Now choose your cognitive distortion(s). Many of us have more than one. Think about how it has influenced your relationships. Remember that once you are aware of your habit you can change it if you want to. The key then is to first become aware of your cognitive distortions. Begin to reframe your thinking. For example, instead of thinking "I am a failure" when something goes wrong, reframe the thought. "The next time I am faced with that choice I'll spend more time thinking about my options."

What you tell yourself will set the direction of your life. Negative beliefs will give you negative outcomes. If you keep telling yourself, "I'm not smart enough, I'm not good enough," your old brain gremlins will agree with you. Brain reprogramming isn't easy. Reprogram your brain, and your feelings will follow. Positive brain messages yield positive feelings, while toxic thoughts are like toxic waste. If your mind is polluted, the direction of your life follows. By cleansing your mind of the negative messages you have reinforced over years you will increase your feelings of self worth. You will value yourself more.

Point of View (POV)

POV is a valuable tool to use and understand when communicating with your marriage partner, with your children, or with your friends and acquaintances. It is the opposite concept to "I win, you lose" or "I'm right, you're wrong." With "I'm right, you're wrong" the loser is once again reduced to a childlike role. The feeling that emerges from this scenario is one of rage, disgust and anger. The winner is no longer loving or loved. If you are wrong often enough you begin looking for an escape route.

Early in my practice sessions with couples I demon-strate point of view by asking each person to name something in the relationship about which they have disagreement or arguments. I ask what the two opinions are about that topic. I ask one of them to sit across from me and place an elbow on the table while I do the same. We grasp hands. I then ask the patient to push as hard as she can while I, in turn, try to push her arm down first. This is a power struggle. While we push I say, "I'm right", and she says "you're wrong." We push and push until one of us lowers the other's arm to the table. Whoever is stronger wins. I do this exercise with each. In almost every case I lose. The next step is to ask them to get into the same position. Only this time the instructions are to allow the arm to be very loose. Just let the arm flip-flop back and forth while holding hands and say the words, "point of view, point of view" (instead of "right and wrong"). There is no power struggle.

With Point of View no one wins, and no one loses. You are entitled to your POV, and I am entitled to my POV. We are two separate people, and have the right to have a different Point of View while still remaining friends.

I have never had a patient miss the point.

<u>Exits</u>

The meaning of exits is that "you are not giving me what I want, so I'll just go away and remove myself from you." Disappointment and anger are at the root of exits.

When couples are unhappy, angry, or dissatisfied with a relationship they find other ways to absent themselves from it. Exiting is giving up, with the most obvious method being divorce. However, you may decide to remain in the marriage for any number of reasons: because your family wouldn't approve; you are frightened to be alone; you cannot economically support yourself; you like your home; you fear there will be violence; and, so on and so on. So you stay! However, in truth you cannot be present for your spouse if you are mentally "checked out": i.e. by watching T.V. alone, playing internet games alone, going to the movies alone, having an affair, using hobbies to escape, or just not talking.

For those who choose to stay married, there are numerous ways to avoid each other: by not engaging in conversation regularly; by refusing to help each other with problem solving; by putting the burden of the marriage on one person or by acting as if you are still single. You cannot be present or engaged when you watch television alone, when you sit in front of the computer playing internet games for hours, when you go to sleep at 8 P.M. while your spouse is putting the children to bed, when you are having an affair or when you use your hobbies to escape. Other exits are playing golf or cards several time a week while your spouse stays at home, joining all kinds of clubs and attending meetings around the time your spouse is returning from work, forever reading the newspaper without comment, reading books and magazines to avoid conversation, and working late at the office every night.

In contrast, when the relationship is working and you feel safe, you laugh together, have good sex together, confide in each other, and trust each other.

To summarize exits, there are many ways that couples stay in the marriage, yet are not there for each other. They stay because of money, family, children, job, laziness, habit, or convenience.

This is not to say that two people have to be together all the time, doing everything together. However, when couples don't want a divorce, even though the marriage is not a happy one, each person devises a method to exist independently. Separation is carried out for the purpose of avoiding each other. It does nothing for marriage communication or for emotional nourishing. Exits separate people.

Another important exit which I haven't discussed is the use of alcohol and drugs to avoid the relationship. These can be street drugs, prescription drugs or recreational drugs.

In this context, drugs are used to numb and deaden marital pain or the pain from the wounds of childhood. When the marriage does not heal those wounds and the relationship feels lifeless, the person's spirit suffers. Depression can then occur, and more drugs are used as medication. Once babies come along, demanding the mother's attention, the needy husband may become resentful and isolated and take his anger out on the children. He may drink and medicate even more to avoid any responsibility in the relationship. The rift becomes wider. The drugs become an obsession and completely separate the user from the partner.

If either partner is addicted to or dependent on drugs (including alcohol), I advise him to get into treatment for the addiction with Alcoholics Anonymous (AA), Narcotics Anonymous (NA) or a rehab clinic. After the person has been in treatment for several weeks I will see the couple for therapy on the condition that the user stay in treatment throughout the work.

An editor of a well-known magazine was quick to tell me that addicted spouses often misused their spouse' history of childhood trauma as a weapon to undermine the work of marriage therapy. He said that because trust is such a big issue for addicts, that marital therapy didn't work for them. My response was that the marriage was already not working, and I quoted the AA motto that, "It will work if you work it."

It is true that couples therapy doesn't succeed for everyone. If the process taught isn't frequently practiced at home, or if one of the partners doesn't want the marriage to succeed, then the therapy will fail. However it is both my personal and professional opinion and experience that many, many marriages are healed through this process. Motivation to succeed is essential.

We've been looking at some of the many ways people think they are protecting themselves, when in fact they are undermining their own happiness. Here is a story of a man who learned his lesson rather quickly. If you can relate to it, learn the lesson. He became a victor instead of a victim.

A man left his apartment to go to work and took the path he always took to get there. That day, while walking, he didn't see an open manhole, and he fell into it. Fortunately he wasn't hurt. He climbed out, brushed himself off and got to work just a few minutes late. The following day, out of habit, he took the same route, and forgetting about the open manhole, he fell into it a second time. Once again he wasn't hurt. He climbed out, brushed himself off and went on to work arriving a few minutes late. On the third day he took a different path.

We've all felt like victims from time to time. Think of a time when you told your "victim story" to anyone who would listen. Tell it to someone again, only this time be a victor instead of a victim. How do you do that?-by taking responsibility for your life. Here are some examples:

Victim version: "My daughter was outside near the pool playing with her toys, and I had to go inside the house and change the baby's diaper. When I went back outside I found that my daughter had fallen into the pool. I quickly put the baby down, jumped into the pool and saved her life. How was I supposed to know she would have fallen in and possibly drowned?"

Victor version: "I needed to change the baby's diaper, but my 3-year-old wanted to stay outside and play near the pool. I insisted that she come inside with me but promised that after I took care of the baby, we would all go out and play at the pool. We did."

Victim version: "Everyone, including my dad, told me to buy this great property. The owner was leaving the country and wanted to sell it quickly. I made an offer, and it was accepted. After I bought it, thinking that I had made a good deal, things started to go wrong with the plumbing and electricity. I found out that the workmanship was inferior, and I had to make expensive replacements. It ended up costing me a fortune. I am so angry at myself and my dad for buying it so fast."

Victor version: "Everyone, including my dad, told me to buy this great property. The owner was leaving the country and was in a hurry to sell, so I made a low offer contingent on having an inspection of the electricity and plumbing. When I got the report back, I cancelled the offer. That would have been a costly disaster".

Victim: "I got married three years ago to Mary. We had lots of fun together, and the sex was great. Now, she's not interested in sex, and all I do is work, work, work, watch T.V. and drink my wine. She doesn't pay attention to me anymore. We're in a rut."

Victor: "I got married three years ago to Mary. We had fun together, and the sex was great. We used to go to the beach, play tennis, ride our bikes and go to the gym. Now, even though we're both busy, we make sure we plan some fun time every week. I also compliment her often and remember to tell her how glad I am that we got married. We talk to each other to find out how things are going and even make dates for sex."

What are your payoffs for having a victim mentality? Do people give you more sympathy? Do they pay attention to you more?

You can play out your marriage choice by being a victim, or you can take responsibility for making the marriage work. It is your choice.

EXITS

? WHAT ARE YOURS ?

1.   2.   3.

4.   5.

My wife says I never listen or something like that.

CHAPTER 9

Explaining Procedures That Work

Method

Let's get started with the therapeutic method. What happens when someone calls for an appointment? Each therapist has his own procedures and rationalizations for why he does things one way and not another. My way is to ask the potential client if her partner knows that she is calling, and if the spouse is agreeable to coming in a minimum of once a week for therapy. I also tell her that, on average, the therapy will continue with me for three months. I say that homework is given each week, and is to be returned at the next session. The three of us can then share the information together.

The prospective client is told that the sessions are between an hour and an hour and a half long. If there are children they may not come into the therapy room during our sessions. The client is asked to commit to not exiting the relationship for at least three months. I ask that each person see me once alone before I see them together. The purpose of the solo meeting is to obtain a history, and after that one time, I will not see them alone except for emergencies and only with the partner's permission. Couples are to arrive at sessions together, and if one arrives before the other he will be asked to wait in the waiting room until the partner arrives. The final instruction is that they are not to use alcohol or drugs for 24 hours prior to their session (unless it is for medical reasons). I explain that there is a daily three-step exercise that must be practiced. I then answer any of the client's questions. The most common question is why they always have to come into the session together. I explain that trust is a big issue at this stage, and it is important that neither party feel that the therapist is showing favoritism to the other.

I encourage clients to call or e-mail me if they have a question between sessions for the purpose of clarification related to the procedure.

The life history, taken separately, is very important. Couples may be married for many years yet know very little about their spouse's childhood. It is important in couples work that there be no secrets related to the way a partner was raised, since it directly affects how their marriage functions and what we do in session.

History-taking covers traumas, illnesses, mental health, incarcerations, medications, addictions, work, education, prior therapy, sexual history, relationships between family members, prior romantic relationships, children and marital history.

Session two introduces principles and goals. Couples are shown the drawing of the circle with the opening. The principle of the unclosed circle is explained. Couples are introduced to the idea that often relationships begin in utero, in the crib, or in early childhood : that it is not an accident that they are together. Why? The couple wants to get from each other what they positively or negatively experienced in childhood.

I give examples below.

1. Allen and Sybil were in their fifties. Each had been divorced and were celebrating their tenth year together. Allen was the middle child of fourteen brothers and sisters. Sybil was an only child. When Allen was asked about his early childhood, he responded that no one paid attention to him. He said he did what was necessary to survive. Sybil, however, was the focus of parental attention and was raised in a happy home.

Allen, unconsciously, chose Sybil because she gave him the attention he craved and was an active partner in his life. In return, she felt attracted to Allen, because he was so attentive, verbal and caring: something she had always experienced growing up.

2. Jean's father was not an affectionate man. She unconsciously chose Joe to fill that childhood gap, yet never felt that Joe gave her enough affection.

3. When Tim wanted to talk, his mother made herself available to him. Tim chose a woman whom he thought was like his mother, only to find that his wife's other interests, after marriage, interfered with their time together.

It is explained that these are usually not conscious choices: that until a couple learns how to communicate effectively, they will only repeat the same mistakes they have been making in their marriage again and again. Emphasis is placed on practicing the process often- everyday, when possible and to not make excuses about doing the homework.

The following tenets of the therapy are introduced:

1. They are not to verbally abuse each other (examples are given).
2. They are not to use physical force.
3. They are not to undermine the therapy by refusing to practice the process between sessions.

Couples are reminded that each person had a life before they met, and that each is in charge of his own life now.

They are reminded of the difference between having to prove one person is right and one is wrong and acknowledging that one person's point of view may be different from his partner's.

They are introduced to the concept of defense mechanisms and how people use them to protect themselves from getting hurt.

They learn about cognitive distortions and how self-limiting they are.

Couples are reminded that their partner is not their parent nor their caretaker.

Both people are asked to sign a contract in which they pledge not to exit the relationship for three months.

Couples are reassured that many relationships can and will be healed as long as they frequently practice the process, do the homework, attend the therapy sessions every week and live up to their signed contract.

It is rare that even the most diligent couple will not occasionally fall back into old, familiar patterns during the learning process. Intellectually, they hear the words and understand them. Emotionally, they react out of habit and attempt to get the therapist to take sides and to support their point of view. When this happens the therapist's job is to model the three steps of the process and to coach the couple to work the program. It takes several sessions before the couple begins to understand that the therapist will not undermine them by falling into the trap of taking sides or getting caught up in a disagreement.

In spite of carefully explained procedures coming from the new brain, the old brain sometimes haunts the proceedings. When this occurs, the result is that, after two or three sessions, some couples drop out. When they call to cancel the message is, "We are going back to the system we are used to and will try to settle it ourselves." In these instances it is clear that nobody is listening. They are too busy making excuses and running away.

The good news is that at least half the couples, with whom I work, rebuild their marriages and go on to heal each other, themselves and their children.

COGNITIVE DISTORTIONS

EVENT	THOUGHT	FEELING
Tonight she is refusing sex	She hates sex	Disappointment and anger
He didn't fix the chair	He's lazy	Disgusted
Talks about former relationship	He misses her	Jealous
Works late too often	Boring man	Guilty

CHAPTER 10

The Three-Step Process

Do my patients really listen to me? Do my patients really hear me?

We all want a sympathetic ear. People are too busy getting hit with visual images: TV, computer screens, fast traffic, movies, cell phone screens, as examples. We need and want someone to hear us, so we know they care. The key is not to talk, talk, talk and then blame one another for something. That's a turnoff. We want to be recognized and acknowledged.

Pretending to listen to a partner by staring at her and remaining silent is not listening. In that case pretending to listen is tolerating your partner.

A good definition of listening is being ACTIVE: paying attention, walking in your partner's shoes, being interested in her as a person, empathizing with the message. The person doing the talking however, can't talk to criticize, interrupt, yell, look angry, demean, and expect to be listened to. In that situation, the listener will shut down, yell back, get angry, walk away.

Is that what your "discussions" are like now? The cliché, "It takes two to tango" means that if you want to be listened to, then speak with sincerity, with thoughtfulness, with kindness, with love, even intensely, but without the shouting and shooting the listener down. After all, it hurts not to be listened to.

2

LISTEN…..MIRROR…..VALIDATE…..EMPATHIZE

LISTEN CAREFULLY AND PUT ASIDE YOUR OWN CONCERNS FOR NOW.

MIRROR WHAT YOU HEAR BECAUSE YOUR PARTNER IS WORTH LISTENING TO. HE KNOWS YOU RECEIVED THE MESSAGE.

VALIDATE WHAT YOU HEAR. THE PERSON SPEAKING HAS A RIGHT TO HER OWN POINT OF VIEW. PUT YOURSELF IN YOUR PARTNER'S PLACE, AND LET HER KNOW YOU FEEL TEIE IMPORTANCE OF THE MESSAGE.

Make it worth his while to listen. PROTECT HIS FEELINGS SO HE DOESN'T WANT TO RUN AWAY!

Anxious, timid, or shy spouses often suffer silently, while assertive or arrogant spouses often explode when something bothers them. The three steps offer a communication alternative which doesn't intimidate the listener. We have to be willing to expose ourselves and to share our thoughts in a safe environment if we want our partner to understand and know us. This therapy is about closing old wounds, not rubbing noses in them. The three steps are:

1. Mirroring
2. Validating
3. Empathizing

Step 1: Mirroring

Mirroring is love in action. Mirroring helps us reveal our experiences to the person we care about, rather than flailing about and being afraid to reveal who we are. Its purpose is to rebuild love through the openness of revelation. Mirroring allows our partner to know that we are really listening and paying close attention to what he is saying. The essence of mirroring is to allow one partner to focus on what the other is saying, and hear without judging. So often, when we speak to one another, we are so busy rehearsing in our minds how to defend ourselves and how to respond that we do not listen to the intrinsic meaning and feeling behind the message. With mirroring you are asked to stop the conversation in your head and just pay attention to what your partner is saying.

Let's look at Tim and Ann. Something is bothering Ann, and she asks Tim if this is a good time to speak to him about it. Tim agrees that this time is convenient. (If the time is not convenient he tells her when it would be a better time that day to have the conversation.) What he does not do is avoid her. When they sit down to talk they sit across from each other. Ann has learned to present what she is saying a sentence or two at a time, and begins to tell Tim why she is upset with something he said or did (or didn't do). The reason she speaks a sentence or two at a time is to be certain that he not only hears her but can remember what she presented. Tim's job is to listen and repeat the message. If he gets the meaning of what Ann said she will continue to talk. She speaks, and he repeats. He can also paraphrase, as long as he tells her the meaning of what she said. Tim doesn't judge or defend himself. He listens. There are no "yeah, buts" or "that is not what I said" or "if you hadn't" – he just LISTENS. What Ann does is to present her point of view and her feelings about the incident without criticism or rebuke. When she finishes what she is saying, Tim asks, "is there more?" and "did I get it all?" until Ann indicates that she is finished.

Finally, Tim's job is to summarize what Ann said. After he does this he asks her if he got it all. If he didn't, she repeats what has been left out and Tim repeats the summary.

When the process begins it feels and sounds mechanical. However over a period of a couple of weeks, and with lots of practice, the process takes on a fluidity that is lacking in the beginning. The homework sheets also help to remind the couple of the steps.

It is essential that the therapist be part of the coaching process during the session. To facilitate I demonstrate when necessary, by role-playing one of the partners. There is also a chart posted nearby with the mirroring procedure on it for the couple's reference until they master the process. Couples will often glance at the chart during the practice to assist them with the procedure. When they wander I remind them of the boundaries. I sometimes hold up a stop sign when it is important to get them back on track. It is only natural in the beginning for the listener to respond by wanting to defend herself or interrupt or give her point of view or sulk. It takes time to teach the couple how to listen to each other and to concentrate on the message without blaming, without judging and without defending.

This process teaches a new way of communicating with a significant other. It conveys ideas and feelings and doesn't dehumanize a partner. Mirroring feels safe. Couples can bring up problems while eliminating the threat of reprisal. When couples use this process consistently, healing begins to occur. Mirroring is practiced until it is comfortable to both.

To recap, I say to the couple, "We are going to use a process that is safe. There will be no insults, no blame, and no shame. The three of us will work together so that you can begin to trust that you will not be hurt or injured. If you react to what XXX says or if you have feelings and thoughts about it, instead of expressing it as you have in the past, I want you to repeat exactly what she says as if you are a mirror. Just repeat it. And when your partner has finished, ask if there is more."

"Finally when the answer is 'no, there is no more,' summarize all of it either exactly, or with paraphrasing, as long as you get the essential meaning. If something is forgotten your partner will repeat what was left out to help you get all of it."

Mirroring is the first step and needs to be practiced until the therapist sees and hears a relatively comfortable presentation. This will require at least a couple of sessions with the therapist, in addition to practicing the process at home a minimum of four days a week. If the practice at home is avoided, it can take several more office sessions to master which means valuable time can be lost. Ideally the couple practices at home every day.

Mirroring is a new and unique way of communicating about topics that are important to one or both of them. There is no yelling, no angry silence, and no criticism once the process is learned. Very often a spouse expresses surprise to learn the deep feeling that is communicated. That's because he is paying attention by listening.

Step 2: Validation

Validation is the step where the "listening" partner confirms that what the "speaking" partner said makes sense. It doesn't mean that the listening partner necessarily agrees with what is heard. Validation is not saying, "you are right". Rather it conveys that, "I see your point of view. What you said makes sense to me." It means she recognizes that POV is being expressed with regard to a particular experience. "I can understand why you feel that way," is another way the listener can respond. Or, "When I didn't keep my word it probably reminded you of how you felt when you were ignored as a little girl." Remember that the injuries and hurts the partners experienced as young children affects their adult behavior and interpretations. That knowledge can now be verbalized in the validation process.

Validation is begun after the mirroring step and feels comfortable. The person who mirrored the message is also the person who validates.

To illustrate validation, our couple Ann and Tim would say something like the following:

Tim: "I understand that you were upset with me for coming home late and not calling you. It is reasonable that you were worried about me after not hearing from me for more than two hours after the time I usually get home. I promise to call you if this happens again."
Ann: "Thank you honey."

There is again a chart posted with examples to assist the couple with the process. While validation is being practiced in session the therapist is there to guide and model this step when necessary. The homework now consists of practicing step one and step two everyday, or at least for a minimum of four days a week.

Step 3: Empathy

Empathy is a powerful step. When we practice putting ourselves in our partner's place when he is hurt, afraid or disappointed, we are practicing reassuring love. This step demonstrates compassion for your partner's feelings and encourages the listener to put herself in the partner's shoes. Words like, "I imagine you must feel…" or "you must have felt really hurt…" or "I am so sorry you felt that way" are often spoken. Sometimes the listening partner is able to associate what she heard with what she learned about the partner's caretakers. For example, if abandonment was a major issue she might say, "not calling you when I was going to be very late at work must have reminded you of being a latchkey kid, when you never knew when your mom was coming home. I can see why you were anxious."

The partner who initially requested the meeting gives brief acknowledgment to the listening partner. This might be a smile, eye contact, "thank you" and even a hug.

After the three steps are completed, roles can be reversed and the listening partner can become the presenter if she so chooses. It is then that the presenter has the opportunity to give his point of view while the other person listens.

To summarize the purpose of the three steps:

The couple is learning to talk to each other and feel safe while doing it. The listening partner is giving her full attention to the speaker. The speaker speaks about her feelings, her impressions, her POV. There is no criticism or attacking. A primary question that is raised by the therapist during this process is, "Did you ever experience these feelings as a child?"

MIRROR—SUMMARIZE—VALIDATE—EMPATHIZE

MIRRORING   "WHAT I HEAR YOU SAY IS..."

SUMMARIZING   "I THINK I GOT IT. WHAT YOU
                   SAID..."

VALIDATING   "I UNDERSTAND, AND IT
                   MAKES SENSE."

EMPATHIZING   "I CAN JUST IMAGINE HOW
                   YOU FELT."

                           OR

                   MAYBE IT REMINDS YOU OF
                   THE TIME WHEN YOU WERE
                   YOUNGER...

                   "CAN WE SWITCH NOW SO I
                   CAN HAVE A TURN TO GIVE
                   YOU MY POINT OF VIEW?"

While mirroring and validation are more a meeting of the minds, empathy is a meeting of the souls. This process is not a quick fix; it takes at least three months of practice before it moves from a mechanical process to a smooth and natural process. Old patterns of communication are habits that developed over time.

These patterns are frequently imitations of what children saw and heard growing up. The habits are difficult to break unless there is awareness, commitment and repetition on the part of both people. It takes patience to practice POV when you want to be right and are used to blaming. It takes awareness to recognize when you begin to revert to old habits such as defending yourself. It takes affection, caring and love to want communication to change for the better.

Observing how couples undermine their own growth during this process is sometimes startling to watch. Earlier I explained that when the phone call first comes through to the office and an appointment is requested, I go over the procedures. One procedure relates to homework assigned at each session. The homework includes practicing the process every day, or a minimum of four days a week, in addition to whenever communication has gone awry. Inevitably some couples will come into session and say they couldn't do their homework because "we were so busy" or "we had company" or "there was no time" or "I was too tired" or "I wasn't ready."

Avoidance is common. Or, one of the partners will plop down at the beginning of a session and say "this isn't working." When questioned about the practice sessions at home he will respond "we didn't do it." It is almost as if they are addicted to their old failed system.

Nevertheless, in session, with a coach, they will do the exercise and reach a satisfactory solution to the presented problem. This is why it often takes several months of work to achieve success. Again, the A.A. motto applies: "It'll work if you work it."

Every couple with whom I've initially spoken is quick to say they want help because of poor communication. There is no special trick, no magic wand to change old family patterns of communication. Focused listening, giving validation and expressing soulful empathy require practice. Rehearsal and motivation are the two components that will make it work. Couples who are passionate about saving a marriage will do the work and be successful. A therapist cannot make it happen. A coach cannot make it happen. A therapist-coach can be a nurturing guide to encourage, to teach, to model, and to plant that dream.

LISTENING: Do you listen? (impatiently) So you can get to say what YOU want to say? Are you practicing inside your head how to respond instead of hearing what your partner is saying? Are you putting on symbolic earmuffs while your brain is full of silent judgment? Are you busy defending yourself silently, rehearsing your comeback, blaming or denigrating him silently? Are you thinking, saying to yourself or out loud, 'when will she ever finish?" Do you listen to him as if he matters?

EMPATHIZING

THERE IS HEALING TAKING PLACE IF HE CAN PUT HIMSELF IN YOUR SHOES.

THERE IS HEALING TAKING PLACE IF SHE CAN PUT HERSELF IN YOUR SHOES.

REMEMBER

NO BLAME!

NO CRITICISM!

NO FORCE!

GIVE PLENTY OF SAFETY!

WHY?

BECAUSE YOU AND THE UNIVERSE CARED ENOUGH TO CHOOSE HER AS YOUR PARTNER. NOW YOU HAVE THE OPPORTUNITY TO GIVE AND GET THE LOVE YOU ALWAYS DREAMED OF HAVING.

CHAPTER 11

Couples Communication

Conflict is not why marriages stop working: it's the silence and slow cumulative anger that destroys a marriage.

<u>LISTEN-MIRROR-EMPATHIZE</u>

Communication takes many forms. It is the way we look at each other, the way our bodies move in each other's presence, the silence between us, the way we speak to each other, our choice of words, the volume of our voice, our gestures or lack thereof, our timing and our exits. Most communication is non-verbal. Even that empty feeling we get when we tune out is communication. Verbal communication requires a voice and an ear. When a wife says, "he doesn't communicate with me," she is thinking of spoken language.

When babies want something they communicate by screaming. They don't smile and say, "Mommy, feed me. I'm hungry" or "please change my messy diaper." For most babies, screaming gets them what they want. Here comes the unconscious old brain again.

Fast forward a few years. Now, that child is grown up and married, and the romantic period of the marriage is over. The old brain says, "scream for what you want," so they scream but don't get it. That method doesn't work anymore. Spoken language is now needed coming from the new brain.

Most of us aren't psychics or mind readers. We've been given the gift of language. We need to tell our partners what we want. In fact, it is impossible for people not to communicate, whether it is by remaining silent, shouting, exiting, speaking or whispering.

This is a process that requires relearning how to communicate in a manner quite different from what we are used to. Once learned it becomes an automatic and smooth process.

Let's look again at the communication between couples:

Lynn detested the anger she was subjected to by her stepfather, and this is why she was attracted to her husband. He was a mild-mannered man seemingly unlike her step-father, and therefore safe. Still, Lynn was very good at unconsciously stimulating anger in her partner in order to work through her unfinished business from childhood.

Bill and Lynn had been married for three years and were in their mid-twenties when they sought my help. Lynn was college-educated and Bill was beginning college. Both worked. They were two months into therapy, which they attended once a week, when I asked permission to record one of their sessions. Here is an excerpt from it:

> Bill: Lynn, I would like to talk to you about our relationship. Is that okay?

> Lynn: Yes, this is a good time.

Lorraine Wincor

PERSON A HAS A SITUATION SHE WANTS TO
TALK ABOUT.

PERSON B HAS AGREED TO SIT DOWN AND
LISTEN TO HER.

PERSON A, IN ONE OR TWO SENTENCES AT A
TIME, SPEAKS ABOUT SOMETHING THAT IS
IMPORTANT TO HER AND THAT SHE WANTS TO
GO OVER WITH HER PARTNER. IT COULD BE
SOMETHING SHE FEELS UNCOMFORTABLE
ABOUT, UNHAPPY ABOUT, OF CONCERN TO HER
ABOUT THE CHILDREN, HER PARTNER, HERSELF.

EXAMPLE: "I WOULD APPRECIATE IT IF YOU
WOULD TALK TO ME AT BREAKFAST. I FEEL LEFT
OUT EATING BREAKFAST IN SILENCE WHILE YOU
READ THE NEWSPAPER EVERY MORNING. I FEEL
LONELY."

Bill: You know that I just came back from China. This week, after I got back, you spent a lot of time with your family. I know you don't see them often, but you were not with me when I got back. You were running around with your family all the time.

Lynn: What I hear you say is ... (*Lynn mirrors what Bill said.*) Did I get it all? Is there anything else?

Bill: I know you asked me to go with you to see your family, but you had already decided to go, whether I went or not. It was after the fact. We didn't plan it together, even though you invited me.

Lynn: (*Mirrors what Bill said.*)

Bill: I worked hard all week, and we hadn't spent any real time together. And you were with your family every day. But you just wanted to be with them. It made me feel angry.

Lynn: (*Mirrors what Bill said.*) Is there anything else?

Bill: I would like to make love <u>with</u> you, not alone. I would like sex with you twice a week. But I feel you are the type of woman who doesn't like sex. You were not that way when we married. I am angry and hurt. I don't want to live this way anymore.

Lynn: (*Mirrors what Bill said.*) Did I get it all? I don't understand.

Doctor: Tell her again, so she can understand that last part.

Bill: (*Repeats what he said about sex.*)

Lynn: (*Mirrors back what Bill said*). Did I get it all?

Lynn: (*Summarizes everything Bill has said. She hasn't left anything out so Bill doesn't have to repeat anything.*)

Lynn (*validates Bill by saying the following*): I understand that you felt left out because I spent so much time with my family. I understand that you wanted to spend more time with me since you were away and had just gotten back. I understand that you feel lonely because I wasn't interested in having sex and that you feel badly for having sex with me when I was asleep.

I do understand that because of my behavior you think I am just not interested in having sex with you. I am sorry that you feel that way, and we do have to talk more about that. The next time my family plans to visit we will have to talk about it more together and make plans that we both agree to.

I'm sorry that I hurt you. You must feel lonely, unloved and angry with me.

Doctor: Remind me again how long you have known each other?

Lynn: We've known each other for five years and have been married for three years. At first the sex was fun and exciting, but now we are both so busy and I am tired all the time with school and work. I am bored with sex now.

Doctor: Do you remember when you first came to see me, I explained to you that when couples are first attracted to each other, they feel super-romantic and very sexual? It is called the "romantic phase" of a relationship and usually lasts about a year. During this period, the couple can't get enough of each other. However, after a while, with school, work, family, other responsibilities getting in the way, life becomes busier and more routine. There is less excitement. That isn't unusual.

In the beginning, we see only the positives in our lover. After a while, we begin to see some negatives and start trying to change the person. We begin making demands and feel less satisfied. We tend to forget the gift our partner has given us by being in our life. It now takes more effort to please each other. At this point, it is easier to fall out of romantic love. That's the reason couples start exiting the relationship.

Lynn, is sleep one of your exits? You know when Bill gets home from work, you are always asleep. And Bill, is avoidance one of your defense mechanisms? When you want to punish Lynn, you frequently get home much later than she expects you to. Can you see how this might get in the way of romance? What do you think? Can you remember, Lynn, how your avoidance worked for you as a child when you were afraid of your stepfather? You stayed out of his way as much as you could, often playing in your room or taking a nap. Is sleep your way of avoiding Bill now?

As romantic love lessens, we start re-injuring each other's childhood wounds and project our negative traits onto our partner. You are blaming Bill for abandoning you when your family was here. Are you punishing him by denying him sex? Is that a possibility? You don't sound angry, Lynn, but is it possible that you are angry at Bill? You felt abandoned as a child, and now your behavior is encouraging Bill to abandon you.

Lynn: Can I have an appointment with you now Bill?

Bill: Yes, now is a good time.

Lynn: My family doesn't visit very often, and I was disappointed and angry that you didn't come with me even on the days you had off from work.

Bill: (*Mirrors it back.*)

Lynn: You say you want to spend more time with me, but then you didn't come with me. They were expecting you. I told them you were coming. I felt abandoned.

Bill: (*Mirrors it back.*)

Lynn: And then the sex thing. When I do want to have sex, you look at me like it's a joke, and then I don't want to. You know how self-conscious I am about my body. It makes me feel bad. I feel rejected again.

Bill: (*Mirrors it back.*) Did I get it all?

Lynn: (*Nods yes.*)

Bill (*validates Lynn by saying the following*): So what I hear you say is that you feel rejected and self-conscious when you ask for sex, and I think it's a joke. And you wanted to be with me when your family was here. And you were disappointed and felt abandoned, as if I am your mother and stepfather. Am I right?

Lynn: (*Nods yes.*)

Bill (*empathizes*): I can imagine that you feel really bad when I act that way, and I am sorry you felt alone and angry. I'm sorry I made you feel that way.

Doctor: Let me interrupt and clarify something. Bill, you did not make Lynn feel that way. Lynn's feelings are hers. She feels the way she feels because of her early experiences of being rejected by her caretakers when she was a little girl. It is her history. What you are sorry about is that she feels that way, not that you made her feel that way. She has a choice now about her feelings, just as you do.

Remember Lynn when we talked about cognitive distortions? And you identified what yours were? Bill, Lynn looks in the mirror and sees her body as faulty, though you and many people tell her she has a great body. The way she sees herself and thinks about herself, is her cognitive distortion, stemming from her mistreatment as a young child. You cannot make her feel anything. Remember that each of us is responsible for the way we feel. Let's try the empathy step again.

Bill: I'm sorry that you feel that way. I love you. I think your body is beautiful.

Doctor: Bill, what do you really want? Let Lynn know, using the process. What do you want, Bill?

Bill: When you come home from work it is late, and you shower and go to sleep. I want some time with you. I've been alone all week.

Lynn: (*Mirrors what Bill said.*)

Bill: When I come home from work, I want to talk with you, even if it is only for ten minutes before you go to sleep. At least one day a week, I'd like you to spend time with me. I'd like to have sex with you twice a week.

Lynn: (*Giggles and laughs as a way of avoiding the subject of sex. Then she repeats the message.*)

Bill: Am I asking too much? I want to spend quality time with you when I get home from work, even if it is only for ten minutes. I want to hold you in my arms and go to sleep with you. I know you have had a long day, and that you are tired, but I want to be close to my wife.

Lynn: (*Giggles.*) You're asking if you are asking too much. You want to spend time with me when you get home even for ten minutes and fall asleep with me so you can be close to me. Did I get it all?

Doctor: Let's dialogue with Bill, Lynn. Are you doing what you did as a little girl? Remember how you ran away and hid when you felt alone?

Lynn: (*Repeats what Bill has said.*) Did I get it all?

Lynn: (*Summarizes everything Bill has presented and checks with him to be certain she didn't forget anything.*)

Lynn (*Validates*): I see your point of view Bill. We need to talk about this more at home and get it straightened out. I love you, and I want this to work better.

Lynn (*Empathizes, but not with much feeling.*) Bill, I realize you feel deprived about the sex, and I feel badly for you. We will have to talk more and make this work.

Bill: I need to keep talking Lynn. Is that okay?

Lynn: (*Nods yes.*)

Bill: I don't feel loved or that you find me attractive.

Lynn: (*Mirrors and validates*): I am so sorry you feel that way. I don't want you to feel that way, but I understand that you do. I want to make a commitment to you that before I go to sleep every night, I will spend time talking to you for at least ten minutes.

Lynn.: (*Empathizes with Bill regarding his feelings of being ignored.*) It must be lonely for you to come home and find me sleeping every night. But I can't make a commitment to have sex with you twice a week. It's too boring.

At this point they had been working for an hour and a half, and we had to stop. They were given a homework assignment. Both of them, in addition to practicing at home, were asked to visit a library, a bookstore or the internet together and research books on sexual games and techniques for the purpose of experimenting and playing together. Along with this they were to process conversations relating to sex. Lastly they were to have some FUN.

Lynn and Bill were asked to practice the process at home related to the sex issue, and one of them was to call me before their next session regarding any difficulty they may have had resolving it.

Lynn called the next day and told me the issue had been resolved. She disclosed to Bill her early memories of her family's attitudes, negativity and inhibitions regarding sexual issues. "They were so uptight about sex and always making negative remarks about sex. I got to the point where I regarded sex as being necessary but dirty, and I didn't feel interested. I realize that I have some work to do on this, and I want to change because I love my husband and this is important to him."

Fortunately Lynn was also seeing a therapist for her individual issues.

Two weeks went by before Lynn and Bill's next session, which turned out to be their last. Their insurance benefits had run out. Lynn and Bill had first called me three months earlier. Their ability to understand how their history impacted on their marriage and their ability to problem-solve by using the process was now comfortable for them. They left the office with new skills in place and holding hands.

Another couple with whom I worked, at the time I wrote this book, dramatically illustrates how the old brain operates in choosing our partners. Remember that the unconscious brain holds the memories of our unmet childhood needs. The husband and wife in this illustration, have large gaps in their open circles.

Ola and Mike came to America from Eastern Europe. They had dated prior to coming to the United States. Five years earlier they married, and when I met them they had two beautiful, healthy children, ages four and two. Mike came to the United States to study and work. Both he and Ola were in their early thirties, spoke fluent English and presented as a handsome couple. While Ola had an MBA, she preferred to be a mother and housekeeper at that time in her life. Ola was seeing a therapist for individual counseling. Mike had a responsible position in the medical field. They owned a home, a boat and two new cars. Their finances appeared secure. Their families resided in Europe, and they had no close friends in the United States. Ola's parents were divorced and Mike's parents had been married for many years.

When Ola called for the first appointment, she said her husband had agreed to couples' therapy, although three prior attempts had failed. I explained my procedures, and we made an appointment. She called that evening to say Mike would come in first for the history-taking.

Mike arrived and quickly announced that he thought he wanted a divorce; this was his "last stand." His history revealed that he came from a family where his father was under the complete domination of a hostile, critical wife. "Once a month, when he can't stand it anymore, he goes out with the boys and gets hammered. He is a beaten-down dog." Mike had a married younger brother with whom he was friendly, but rarely saw. He revealed that his mother never gave affection and was demeaning and critical of everything Mike did from early childhood to the present. She also disapproved of any woman he ever dated. There was nothing positive that Mike could report about his mother. He never saw affection displayed between his parents or towards their children.

Ola's history-taking revealed a family history that was also extremely troubled. Her father was an abusive drunk. While her mother was supportive of Ola, she was unable to protect her from abuse. Ola lived in terror through most of her childhood. Her mother finally left her father, taking Ola with her, and she felt safe for the first time in her life. Unfortunately, and much to Ola's dismay, her mother returned to live with her father after a couple of months, and Ola had no choice but to accompany her. The intense fear returned. She also felt much anger against her mother for going back. The drinking and abuse continued. Ola's only support system was her maternal grandparents. On the rare occasions when she was with them, she felt safe.

It was clear that these two attractive, intelligent people were playing out their early childhood trauma with each other. Mike was full of rage, all of which was displaced onto his wife Ola, who became frightened and submissive. Mike could easily control Ola. For example, even though she had an MBA degree, he took charge of all the family's finances without consulting her. When he yelled, as he frequently did, she cowered.

He was addicted to rage, as was her father. When Mike yelled, Ola shut down just as she did as a child. Her only defense was to withdraw and exit the relationship.

In sessions following the interviews Mike refused to look at her or address her by anything except "she." He refused to practice the process at home, saying he wasn't available. In session he would consistently try to manipulate and try to structure everything his own way. His wife, according to him, was always at fault. When exercises were rehearsed, Ola threw herself into them, demonstrating to Mike her willingness to give him positive feedback. Mike would not be influenced, refusing any physical touch or support for her.

After two months of weekly sessions Mike announced that he thought things were getting a little better at home, and Ola agreed with him. I felt hopeful. Then he made a shocking announcement. He had invited his parents to visit for two weeks without consulting his wife. Ola was devastated. She anticipated that, as always, there would be friction and misunderstandings leading to major arguments. She didn't want the children subjected to those scenes. Mike asked me to help them prepare for the visit.

We went into great detail about how that visit should be set up and what messages he had to convey to his parents regarding their behavior during the visit. Mike was asked to write the ideas down and to rehearse them with Ola. There was much tension in anticipation of that visit. They cancelled their therapy sessions for the two weeks of the visit and promised to call me if they wanted help.

I heard nothing for two weeks, and then they returned. The first week went relatively well, they said. The second week was a disaster. Mike took his parents out every day, leaving Ola and the children at home. The progress, they thought they had made, collapsed. It was like starting all over again. Mike was still finding excuses for not doing the homework and blaming Ola. He played the victim with great consistency, always reporting how confused and troubled he was by Ola's behavior. She remained silent during these attacks.

Breaking my rule, I asked Mike, with Ola's permission, to come in for a session alone. I advised him that he needed an individual therapist, and I gave him several names. He agreed with me and said he would call one. My other suggestion to Mike was that he enroll in an anger management program at the addiction center near his home. I advised him that a mere three months, given all that had disrupted their progress, was not enough time for couples' therapy to be effective. I agreed to see them again once he had begun his own therapy and after he had completed at least half of the anger management work. They had a double session before their temporary "therapy vacation."

Mike called me between sessions to say that they had been practicing diligently and were going to continue for the next several days prior to their appointment. He appeared to have awakened.

I re-negotiated with Mike and agreed to continue seeing him and Ola as long as he had his own therapist and attended the anger management program. I became hopeful that they would learn how to love each other for themselves and for the sake of their two children.

The lesson here is that intelligence is not enough for success. The new brain can understand the concepts, but the old brain can be resistant to the principles. The hope for Mike was that individual therapy and the anger management program would unlock that resistance. Mike's childhood emotional trauma was so devastating that he was left emotionally crippled. His reptilian brain was encrusted with early messages that he was not worth loving, therefore unlovable. Behaviorally he became his mother, and Ola became a victim. She too was playing out her childhood role by marrying her abusive father. She recognized this. At times she felt paralyzed with fear. Ola was searching for the opening in Mike's resistance to make life better for her, for Mike and the children.

Unless we feel ourselves worthy of love we cannot receive it. When we forgive ourselves our liabilities, as we see them, we can forgive others theirs. Criticizing ourselves makes it easy to criticize others.

The following couple illustrates that age has very little to do with married couples wanting to rediscover love. Maggie and Ted were 75 and 80 years old when I met them. Both had been widowed, and had been friends in their teens and twenties. Maggie's husband and Ted had been business buddies years before, which kept the couple socially connected. But they had lost touch and had not spoken to each other for two decades.

One day Maggie, who lived in Florida, decided to call Ted, who lived in Pennsylvania, to ask how he was.

Ted told her his wife had died. He and Maggie talked for a long time, and he asked her if he could visit. Maggie said yes. A week later Ted arrived at her apartment and never left. They were married six months later. They appeared unaware of their ages and had fallen in love. They behaved like any other smitten couple. Both of them had grown children and grandchildren, and they came to see me before they married to make sure they were doing the right thing. "I wanted to date Maggie when she was in her teens, but her father said she was too young to date," Ted said.

What was unique about their behavior was that they were unabashedly thrilled to show their affection to each other. Ted gazed at Maggie with a look of satisfaction and always with a smile on his face. They held hands and hugged each other. Ted talked about the fun they had exploring restaurants and movies together and how they took long drives and talked about their memories. They appeared non-critical, fun-loving and romantic together. Toward the end of the session we talked about their marriage plans.

I kept in touch with this couple on occasion. Five years after celebrating their lives together Maggie developed Alzheimer's and could no longer remain at home. Ted was devastated that he was unable to care for her. She went into a nursing facility. Ted was then 85 and had cancer and heart disease. For two years they spent every breakfast, lunch and dinner together. He drove to visit her every day, seven days a week, and sat next to her, stroked her, brushed her hair, fed her, kissed her, wheeled her outside for fresh air, and told her jokes she could no longer find amusing.

One day, as he sat beside Maggie, he closed his eyes
and died. She followed him a month later. The nurses
said she was distraught because of his absence. They
loved each other until the end of their lives on earth. At
ages 83 and 88 they knew and experienced what love
was about. We are never too old to love.

CHAPTER 12

Changing For the Good

The work of Dr. Dean Ornish was featured in the *Time* magazine "100" issue on alternative medicine, and he was chosen by *Life* magazine as one of the 50 most influential people of his generation. Dr. Ornish tells us that lifestyle changes heal us because a healthy lifestyle reduces the inflammation which is responsible for all chronic disease. Dr. Ornish believes that if you change your attitudes and beliefs, you change your disease.

I heard a lecture once by holistic cardiologist Dr. Kristine Soly. My interpretation of what Dr. Soly said is that when something with our bodies goes wrong, we heal ourselves 90 percent of the time; faith in our bodies is the best healing we have – better than drugs or a medical procedure. Unconditional love is our most powerful healer and we need to strive to love ourselves and others unconditionally in order to stay healthy. Negative energy causes disease, while positive energy promotes health. Most factors that cause disease stem from our thoughts and beliefs, with hate creating the worst energy, and love the most positive. Throughout life, especially when we are young, things happen to us that we misinterpret and hold onto for decades. These misinterpretations become our false beliefs, and false beliefs in turn create negative conditions which produce pain and disease.

In Dr. Bernard Segal's book *How To Live Between Office Visits*, the doctor discusses asking for help, dealing with anger, confronting destructive images of ourselves and unconditional love.

The therapy I have described is a program that concurs with these medical doctors' points of view. This therapy is a teaching tool that begins with our life history. We are a composite of both multigenerational genes and experience. From conception, many of us are negatively influenced by family, caretakers, culture and experience, leaving some of us vulnerable and needy as adults.

Most of us seek wholeness in our lives. One way we pursue that goal is by marrying the person we believe will give us completion. The initial attraction, aside from the physical, is based on an unconscious and hidden agenda. That agenda is related to our lives with our parents or caretakers from the time, soon after conception, and follows us into adulthood.

Said another way, we are seeking to re-experience those positive and negative aspects of our parents or other caretakers that affected us as children physically, emotionally and spiritually. As adults we want to either feel more of the same, or work through the pain and suffering we formerly experienced. The partners we select have some of the traits we both loathe and love.

As adults we have the opportunity to re-experience and work through the issues we were unable to work through as children, because back then we had neither the knowledge nor the power to do so.

In counseling, the therapist helps couples re-examine the people who raised them, by recalling what they were like, how they behaved and what they stood for in relation to child-raising. The patient recalls memories both good and bad. They are asked what they, as children, feared and loved the most, and what they yearned for and didn't receive. In completing the exercises each sees his partner in a new way. Couples rediscover what they want from each other and what they can give to each other now.

The steps are prescribed and definitive. This is a re-learning process for how to safely communicate and problem-solve important issues in the marriage. The couple is on a journey related to the power of trans-formation. Each spouse re-examines the relationship and learns what to do when a bump or roadblock appears.

While the approach is a positive, changing-for-the-good experience, it can be uncomfortable. The program focuses on a couple's strength. If you are stuck on your own petard, it shows you how to climb off and go in another direction. Until you are comfortable with this new path, you may feel unsafe and unsure of yourself. It takes continued work and practice, to be able to shift patterns of old behavior and is achieved through practice, practice, practice. Couples therapy allows two people to create a vision of what their dream relation-ship would look like, then helps them to formulate a map to get there.

And finally, the program doesn't "fix" people. We are whole persons with past demons to face, and we are taught how to let them go. Strategies are used that will give couples what they say they want. A great deal of rehearsal is needed. The partners are shifting from couple-destructive behavior to couple-successful behavior for the purpose of achieving their vision. This can be the start of a new journey. I ask the couple to climb outside the box that has constricted them, and begin that new journey now.

A young woman marries and her mother calls to ask how the honeymoon went. Her daughter tells her mother is was amazing, exciting, romantic.

"But when we got home, he went crazy – using the worst language I ever heard. He was using nasty 4 letter words, and I want to come home."

"What words?" her mother asked.

"Well, here they are: dust, wash, iron, cook!"

CHAPTER 13

Exercises That Reinforce Success

There are several purposes for these exercises. By practicing them you interact directly with your partner in a "hands-on" mode, and thereby learn more about each other than you already know. It is a way of turning the theory, discussed in the book, into practice. The exercises also offer a way to have fun together while making mutual discoveries.

As with all exercising, it takes frequent practice to develop and strengthen your "muscles," whether they are the emotional muscles of the brain, or those of the heart or biceps. These exercises are meant to increase understanding between two people who want their relationship to flourish.

Note: In all of these exercises, the word "caretaker" generally refers to mother or father. However, given the high rate of divorce, caretaker can also refer to step-parents, grandparents, foster parents, other relatives, and so forth. Please substitute the appropriate term as it applies to your life.

Incomplete Sentences

Here is an example of one couple practicing the exercise. It involves completing sentences for the purpose of learning more about each other's child-hoods. We'll call them Jon and Mary.

Mary: Jon, when you feel anger or disrespect coming from me, who does it remind you of in your childhood home?

Jon: It reminds me of _____
(Jon completes the sentence)

Mary: When you were a small child, what were the three worst memories you have of living with your family?

Jon: My first _____
My second _____
My third _____

Mary: What were your three best memories?
Jon: My first _____
My second _____
My third _____

Jon: Mary, when you think of your dad and you think of me, what do you notice that's similar? Tell me how your father and I are alike. Tell me how we are not alike. Describe what your ideal father would have been like. In other words, what did you want from him that you didn't get?

Mary: The similarities I notice are _____
The dissimilarities are _____

Mary: Jon, when you think of your mother and you think of me, what do you notice that's similar?
What do you notice that is dissimilar? Describe what your ideal mother would have been like. In other

words, what did you want from her that you didn't get?

Jon: The similarities I notice are _____
The dissimilarities are _____

Jon: Mary, ask me to be your dad, and tell your dad in the dialogue process, what you want. Let me, as your dad, mirror you back. See if I can summarize, validate and empathize.

Mary: Jon ask me to be your mother, and tell your mother in the dialogue process what you want from her. Let me, as your mother, mirror you back. Then see if I can summarize, validate and empathize.

<u>I FELT...</u>   <u>I FEEL...</u>

1. Make 2 copies of the lists of negative verbs and positive verbs below.
2. Each of you select some of the + and – words that fit the way you felt <u>as a child</u> when you were around your caretakers.

Now do it again, only this time do it as you feel now around your partner.

When you are finished making your selections, sit across from each other and share the lists. Start each sentence with "I felt..."when you are sharing what it was like with your caretakers and, "I feel" when you are sharing what it is like with your partner. Feel free to expand on the experiences as you share with each other.

This is a good chance to practice the 3 steps of listening, mirroring and empathizing so your relationship can change for the good.

NEGATIVE WORDS

Afraid, annoyed, angry, bored, disgusted, disappointed, dejected, depressed, embarrassed, fearful, frustrated, guilty, hated, hopeless, helpless, hostile, jealous, lonely, miserable, nervous, overwhelmed, pessimistic, resentful, sad, stubborn, threatened, troubled, uncertain, uneasy, useless, upset, worried, worn out, weary,

POSITIVE WORDS

Affectionate, blessed, cheerful, comfortable, concerned, delighted, determined, excited, glad, grateful, happy, joyful, kindly, loved, loving, loyal, peaceful, proud, rested, relieved, relaxed, secure, satisfied, supported, worthy, worthwhile

The Nurturing Exercise

This exercise is a treasure. It is usually practiced after two or three weeks of therapy. The purpose of this exercise is to help release some of the tension, isolation and hurt a child feels when caretakers are absent emotionally and physically. The child is in a safe place now, being held by a life partner who wants to hold her.

Optimally the couple will sit on large pillows arranged on the floor. If that is physically uncomfortable they can sit next to each other on a couch. One partner will begin by agreeing to hold the other. The partner to be held first leans against the partner who will do the holding. The holder embraces his partner as if she is a small child. This is the vulnerable child. The holder's job is to help the child feel safe. The dialogue looks something like this.

Mary: Jon, are you willing to be held?

Jon: Yes, if you are willing to hold me.

Mary: Tell me what you wanted and needed from your caretaker that you didn't get.

Jon: What I wanted was _____.

Mary repeats what was said and asks Jon if there is more until it is complete.

Note: This exercise must not be rushed. It isn't easy to look at old hurts and injuries. The partner holding "the child" needs to have patience and compassion. The holdee will feel whether or not she is being nurtured.

Mary: (acting as his mother) It must have been hard for you to be so little and know that I left you alone so much. You must have felt needy and unloved (*validation*). What did you need most that I was unable to give you? Tell me about your hurt.

Each partner takes a turn being the holder and the holdee. Frequently tears are shed. This can be a very emotional experience for both. It opens up old wounds, yet is valuable, because each partner is sharing and divulging secrets that may have never been discussed.

It allows emotional release. This exercise brings two people closer by revealing intense feelings about their history. It is a healing exercise which touches the hearts of those holding and for those revealing their inner childhood history.

Mary and Jon: What can we do that will take away some of the hurt we are feeling? It must be something that we can measure, like giving three hugs a day, or saying something loving four times a day. What should we ask for? Let's write it down and begin giving these gifts to each other.

Note: It is important to keep a record of gifts promised. If does not work to ask your partner to "love me more," because that is not a measurable request. Whereas if you ask your partner for three hugs a day, that can be counted and a written record can be kept. This has been found to be valuable when beginning new behaviors. Once the new behavior becomes routine it is no longer necessary to measure.

Rainbow Exercise

How many times in the course of a week do you say, "I love your necklace, your dress, your hair, your mustache, your beard, your shirt?" How many times in that period do you say, "I love your smile, I love your deep voice, I love holding your hand, I love sitting close to you?" Is love only below the waist, or does it include features above the neck as well, including thoughts and behaviors?

This exercise is fun! If the true purpose of a marriage is to heal each other, this exercise illustrates the kind of conversation that makes healing a reality. My clients never resist doing this although initially they may appear tentative. This can be played after several weeks of therapy and should be repeated every few weeks.

Partners sit across from each other. Each one takes a turn telling his partner all the things that are desirable about him. This includes appearance, behavior, character traits, things that are appreciated related to gifts of food, sex, attention, and conversation.

"I like your hair, the shape of your eyes." "I like it when you tell me about your day."

Tell your partner as many positive things as you can think of. Expound on all the pleasures of having that person in his or her life. This is what the exercise looks like in actual practice taken from one of Jill and Tom's sessions:

Jill giggles in anticipation.

Tom: "I like your skin and the shape of your face. I like the color of your eyes, the shape of your ears, your long neck, and the color and cut of your hair. I love your straight back and your smile. I love the size of your breasts and their shape. I love the way your waist curves in and the shape of your butt. I love your long legs and how smooth your body feels. I love the hair on your vagina and your wetness."

"I love the way you talk when you are feeling happy. I love the way you take your time and talk to me about problems and ask my advice. I love to see you reading the newspaper and books and sharing with me the parts you like best. I love it when you cuddle with me in bed and how you stroke me when you want me to make love to you."

The same process was repeated with Jill.

The first time this exercise is performed, depending on the state of the relationship in the early part of therapy, the outcome can appear dismal. One husband responded this way:

Ed: "I can't think of anything to say. Well, I like it when you cook for me; and when you clean the house; and when you do the laundry. And, I like it when you take care of the children."

Ed would not say anything else on his first attempt. His wife was more generous when it was her turn. They performed this exercise a month later with better results.

Ed: "I appreciate that you take care of your appearance, that you keep your body clean and your hair and skin smooth and attractive. I like the color of your hair and the way you look at me when we talk. I appreciate your patience when I get angry and your self control in not yelling back at me though you must want to. You are a good and loving mother, always paying attention to the children and protecting them. You are also a very good cook and housekeeper so that I know where to find things. You are considerate most of the time, and you ask me to talk to you and practice the process even when I tell you it isn't the right time. You are patient with me. I hope this was better than a month ago."

ASK FOR PLEASERS

EXAMPLE:

1. Remember that this is his and her POINT OF VIEW (POV): not right or wrong
2. Listen to your partner 10' a day for one week. Just listen and make eye contact
3. Take special care with the children so your spouse can take a bubblebath or go on an errand if he wants to.
4. Give your partner 3 hugs a day...just because
5. Perform a household task you usually don't take the time or interest to do
6. Brush your teeth before you decide to kiss her or him on the mouth
7. Put the toilet seat down after you use it if that's her thing
8. Put away your socks and underwear after she washes your clothes
9. Kiss him goodnight every night for a week as starters
10. Consider making dates for sex and make it fun and satisfying.
11. ADD TO THE LIST WITH YOUR OWN PLEASERS

Write Your Own Contract

The purpose of this exercise is to increase positive thoughts about who you are as a person. In spite of early childhood experiences, low self-esteem, codependency issues, guilt, inhibitions, feelings of unworthiness and past failures (many of which are brought on by cognitive distortions of early childhood). Writing a personal contract allows you to set new goals, empowers you to have attainable dreams and resets your thinking.

Make your contract your daily mantra. Say it when you rise, before you go to sleep, and think of it throughout the day. Put it in a room in your house and read it aloud every day.

If this is the first day of the rest of your life, what do you want it to look like?

If you were the captain of your own boat, would you steer it, or let it go wherever it chose to?

This is your life. Who are you? What do you want? Know yourself first, and the contract is the next step.

Your contract should describe your personal assets. Write it down in your favorite colors on a large sheet of paper in big letters. Hang it up where you can see it every day. Add to it when you think of something new.

Here is an example of one person's contract:

"I am a powerful woman. I am attractive, intelligent, hard-working, honest, loving, friendly, spiritual and believe in a peaceful world. I believe love is the purpose of life, and I will do whatever I can from now on to prove it."

Caring Days

Do you remember the things you did for each other when you first met and were first married?

Write down a list of at least ten positive, specific ways your partner can please you. For example, she can give you a back rub, ride a bike with you, pay you two compliments every day, give you two hugs a day, and smile when you come home.

Commit to doing three to five things for each other every day. Do not fall into the bargaining trap of saying, "I'll do this if you do this." This is not conditional.

You are working together to heal childhood wounds which have lasted you a lifetime. This is your time to soften and heal your hearts.

Remembering

In this game, soft music is essential.
Each partner takes his turn.

Close your eyes and take yourself back to the earliest age that you can remember before the age of ten. Perhaps you are at a picnic, the beach or your back yard, and both parents are there. Remember what you liked best about your mother. Keep it in your mind. Now remember your father or step-father or grandparents or any other important caretaker in your life.

Picture what they looked like, how they behaved, what they might have said to you.

(This is your memory bank and no one else's. Your partner is here to support you to work out those negative and positive memories. It is not an accident that you chose her for this task. You need each other to heal the wounds you might have experienced.)

Now open your eyes, and with a soft heart tell your partner what you experienced and what you remember. Remember that your partner is not the disappointing caretaker you might have experienced as a child. She is a grown-up with unmet childhood needs herself. Together you can help each other. If you want to, take a minute and tell your caretakers that you forgive them now. Let them know that, in spite of what you experienced, you now have a loving and supportive partner.

Requesting a Change For the Better

Once the process is understood and the couple has practiced and is comfortable with listening, mirroring, validation and empathizing, each can ask the other to change a specific annoying or troublesome behavior. Timing is important. By the time couples have used the process successfully and appreciate the progress they have made, some trust has been established and couples feel safer.

Some behaviors are more difficult to change than others. The recommendation, at this point, is that easy changes be requested. Remember that so much has been shared, that the heart has been softened by revealing and empathizing with childhood pain. It is appropriate now to anticipate more understanding from your partner. The requests have to be specific and concrete. Statements like, "I want you to be nicer to me", or "I want you to respect me more", are vague and can't be measured. What does respect mean? Exactly what behaviors do you want performed to show respect? On the other hand, requests like getting home from work by 7 p.m. two nights a week, or receiving three hugs a day are easy, specific and doable requests that demonstrate consideration and empathy.

The partner asking also commits to doing something in return for the request. It doesn't have to cost money if money is an issue. It can be as simple as playing board games together, watching a movie at home, cooking together or enjoying a romantic evening; whatever the creative imagination will allow both of the people to enjoy.

Remember Lynn and Bill? (He wanted her to stay awake long enough to talk to her when he got back from a long work day.) If he were asking for an easy behavior change it might look something like this. "I would like you to be awake when I return from work so we can talk for 10 minutes." For that couple, asking her to stay awake for 10 minutes was an easy request. Asking her to stay awake so that he could make love to her, given her lack of commitment to having sex twice a week, was a hard request at that point. In return for her agreement to stay awake, Bill promised her that he would get home an hour earlier two nights a week.

What is essential in all of this is that we demonstrate our willingness to make positive changes. When Lynn feels ignored in her husband's family home, Bill could help her feel less isolated by touching her shoulder or holding her hand while he communicates with his parents in a language Lynn doesn't understand. Once Bill understood Lynn's childhood abandonment issues and feelings of isolation, it was easy for him to make that shift and change his behavior.

Softening Hearts: A Guided Imagery

This exercise is normally done in a therapist's office with the doctor giving the instructions, but if a couple wishes to do it at home they will need to first record the instructions below on some sort of recording device. Then it can be played back during the exercise to guide the process, in lieu of the therapist. Two stools or chairs are also needed for this exercise.

The couple sits one behind the other, facing in the same direction. Both partners should allow their lips to part slightly and allow their chins to relax, then turn on the recorded instructions, which go as follows:

"Close your eyes. Take three slow, deep breaths, and let each breath out slowly as you say to yourselves 'RELAX' with each exhalation. Feel the breath entering your lungs as you breathe deeply. Feel the breath slowly emptying out of your lungs as you breathe out. Relax and feel comfortable, feel safe. Let your mind relax...emptying out any worries, any concerns, any distracting thoughts. Quiet your mind now..."

"As you continue to breathe in and out, slowly feel the soft air around you as if it is a protective cushion surrounding you and keeping all negativity away. Feeling safe and relaxed, the partner in back is becoming aware of the person in front. Gently place your hands on each shoulder of your partner in front of you. Gently... soft touch ... continue to breathe softly and gently as your hands rest lightly on your partner's shoulders. Your hands are still."

"Sense the burdens that these shoulders carried as a child: the back that may have held pain from disappointment and hurt as a child. RELAX. Allow the warmth of your hands to soothe those shoulders and let that gentle energy from your soft hands spread downward through your partner's back, around to the chest. See that gentle energy spreading down the arms, down the torso, down the legs and feet as your partner's body relaxes more and more, enjoying your caring touch. Your breathing is slow and gentle. Your hands remain still."

"The partner receiving this gift is feeling the caring touch and the energy sent to the body. Picture this energy spreading throughout your body. The gift being sent through those caring hands is sent from the heart. Those hands want you to be healed of all hurts, all misunderstanding, all emotional and physical pain. Let that energy go to any part of the body that needs healing."

"Enjoy this contact, this connection, and whenever you are ready, let the hands of the person in back lower to the lap and feel the healthy energy still surrounding you both. Whenever you are ready slowly open your eyes, take in a soft breath and know that your two hearts are softer and healthier for this experience."

Note: The couple should then exchange places and repeat the exercise, so that each has a chance to be in the front seat and to feel the partner's hands resting on his shoulders.

Your Dream Relationship

How would you like your relationship to be?

Make a list and put it in the present tense. For example:

- We like to go fishing together.
- We like to play at the beach together.
- We like to play with the children.

Remember the things you did together during the early stages of your relationship. Talk about it. Choose your preferences.

Work on the list together. Post it in where you can both see it everyday. Read it aloud once a week on a particular night, perhaps at the table before the food is served.

Remember the things you did together when you were in the romantic phase, and list the ones that will still work now. Add to the list if you want to.

Note: Make a commitment to do one of these activities at least once a week.

Couples' Checklist

Work as a team on this exercise. It's like a report card. If you score a low grade the first time you do it, you can study and practice and raise your grade the next month when you do it again.

Below are statements. Each of you scores each statement according to your point of view. The scores that each of you record, won't always match. Put an 'A' if you agree with the statement completely. Give it a 'B' if it's mostly true. Give it a 'C' if you think it's an area where you are average and can improve. BE HONEST! After you have completed all of them, share it with each other. Remember NO COGNITIVE DISTORTIONS. This is your POV.

We support each other most of the time.

We don't lie to each other.

We are sexually content.

We practice the three steps every week.

We support each other when support is wanted.

We give each other surprises at least once a month

We touch each other lovingly at least once everyday.

We use POV instead of right and wrong.

We are sure to remember to compliment each other at least once each day.

We talk to each other and listen to each other everyday.

We don't use defense mechanisms to escape.

We do not use exits to avoid being with each other.

When we make promises we keep them.

You can add additional columns to the right of the page and date each column so you can track your progress over time. Repeat the exercise once a month and notice if the scoring changes for the better. It should if you are <u>working the process</u>.

Finally, say something nice to your spouse at least once a day.

What to do when you've completed the book:

1. Keep working the program. Do a little everyday.

2. Complete any undone written exercises.

3. Every week do the Holding Exercise until the childhood painful memories are weak or painless.

4. Remember to practice the Rainbow Exercise (p. 102). It nourishes the heart.

5. Complete a written vision of what your dream relationship looks like. Put it up in your home where you can see it everyday. Read it aloud once a week.

6. Visualize and express appreciation that your partner is a gift in your life. Don't just think it - speak it to your partner.

7. See your partner's needs as a chance for you to expand your own vision and grow.

Marriage is when a man and woman become as one: the trouble starts when they try to decide which one.

WEEKLY SESSION PREPARATION FORM

If you are currently in couples counseling, check with your therapist first about using this form.

E-MAIL OR FAX A DAY AHEAD OF YOUR APPOINTMENT.

DATE _____
NAMES _____

To get the most out of your session it is best to spend time together preparing for it. Please dialogue with your spouse or significant other. Decide the following:

What we have accomplished since our last session – our wins and victories:

1. _____
2. _____
3. _____

What we didn't get done and want to be held account- able for:

1. _____
2. _____

What we appreciate and are thankful for:

1. _____
2. _____
3. _____

How we want to use the doctor today and what do we want to get out of the session:

_____

_____

_____

What we commit to doing before the next session

1. _____
2. _____
3. _____

We did our homework and will bring it to the session.

The angry wife met her husband at the door. He had alcohol on his breath and lipstick on his cheek. "How dare you show up at 6 a.m. like this? You'd better have a good reason."

The husband answered, "There is...breakfast!"

BIBLIOGRAPHY

Amen D. (1998) *Change Your Brain, Change Your Life.* Three Rivers Press

Burns D. (1980) *Feeling Good.* Harper Press

Capacchione L. (1991) *Recovery of Your Inner Child.* Simon & Schuster/Fireside

Fonil J (2002) *The 7 Best Things Happy Couples Do.* Health Communications

Freud S. (1969) *An Outline of Psychological Analysis.* WW Norton & Co.

Gottman J (1999) *The 7 Principles for Making Marriage Work.* Three Rivers Press

Harley W. (1994) *His Needs Her Needs.* Revill

Hendrix H. (2007) *Getting The Love You Want.* Henry Holt & Co.

Jeffers S (2007) *Feel The Fear And Do It Anyway* Ballantine Books

Jung C G (1990) *The Undiscovered Self.* Princeton University Press

Lipton B. (2005) *The Biology of Belief.* Mountain of Love/Elite Books.

McClean, P. *Man and His Animal Brain*. Modern Medicine Feb. 1964

Ornish, D. *Intensive Lifestyle Changes For Reversal of Coronary Heart Disease*. IAMA 280. 1998-2001.

Prochaska J., DiClemente C. and Norcross J. *Changing for Good*. Harper Collins 1994.

Restak C. *The Brain Has A Mind of Its Own*. Harmony Books 1991

Siegal B. *Peace, Love & Healing*. Harper Row 1989

Siegall B. *How To Live Between Office Visits*. Harper Collins 1993.

The Marriage Circus is about creating the life you always dreamed of having. After remarrying in 2000, Dr. Wincor and her husband Dr. Reichbach recognized that their communication and problem solving skills left much to be desired. They signed up for an Imago workshop and followed up by seeing an Imago therapist. Dr. Wincor was so impressed with the method that she adopted it into her own practice. She believes it has been highly effective for many of her patients.

Whether you are married, single, heterosexual, homosexual, preparing to marry or seeking a partner, you are a candidate for this method as long as you are committed to working the process.

To contact the author, please visit her website:

www.LorraineWincor.com